THE
WORLD OF
FORMULA 1

THE
WORLD OF
FORMULA 1

DAVID TREMAYNE & ALAN HENRY

HAMLYN

First published in 1989 by
The Hamlyn Publishing Group Limited
a division of The Octopus Publishing Group,
Michelin House, 81 Fulham Road, London SW3 6RB
and distributed for them by
Octopus Distribution Services Limited
Rushden, Northamptonshire NN10 9RZ

ISBN 0 600 567354

Produced by Mandarin Offset
Printed in Hong Kong

PICTURES
Half-title *Gilles Villeneuve (Ferrari): Monaco 1981*

Title spread *Alain Prost (McLaren) leads Patrick Tambay (Renault) and Elio de Angelis (Lotus): Zandvoort 1984*

This spread *Elio de Angelis (Lotus) leads team-mate Ayrton Senna: Montreal 1985*

CONTENTS

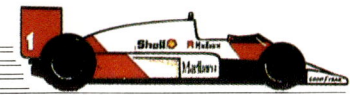

Picture Acknowledgements

All photographs by **LAT PHOTOGRAPHIC**
with the exception of the following:

AllSport/Bernard Asset 130–1
Vandystadt 6 inset;
Colorsport 28, 96 top
Compoint 80–1
de Nombel 6–7;
Nigel Snowdon 8–9

Jacket photographs:
Main photograph: AllSport/Pascal Rondeau
Top right: AllSport/Pascal Rondeau
Above centre: AllSport/Vandystadt-Alain Patrice
Below centre: AllSport/Pascal Rondeau
Bottom right: AllSport/Pascal Rondeau

INTRODUCTION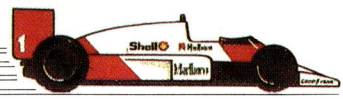

The 1988 season with Honda Marlboro McLaren was fantastic for me, as a newcomer to the team. McLaren have been a dominant force in Formula One for much of the decade – but even for them it was a very special season, with victory in an unprecedented 15 out of 16 races and setting numerous other records.

In F1, getting to the top and staying there is a matter of having the right package – a good design, a well-developed car, a good engine, together with meticulous preparation, reliability, financial support and the total commitment of everyone on the team.

For myself, I particularly enjoy the technical side of Formula One. Our work is at the leading edge of this area of technology, and trying to understand the car and the engine, and trying to analyse and interpret the information as precisely as possible with the team engineers is something I find very rewarding.

The World of Formula One is a vivid account of the turbo decade – one of the most exciting and innovative in Grand Prix history. As World Champion in the final season of turbocharging, I'm delghted to introduce this book to all fans of F1.

Ayrton Senna

Setting the Scene

Preceding two pages
Leyton House March Racing showed how a small team with a state-of-the-art design, Adrian Newey's 881, could make its mark in F1. Team founder, the late Cesare Gariboldi, is in the foreground in dark trousers.

Below Ferrari is racing's oldest established team and its most successful, but it wasn't until Harvey Postlethwaite's 1982 126 C2, seen here in Villeneuve's hands in practice at Long Beach, that it began to harness Eighties technology.

The face of the Grand Prix team has changed a great deal over the years, but the eighties have brought more dramatic change than any other decade.

Now, even though Ferrari is currently the only *grandee* (manufacturer of its own engine and chassis) it is no longer enough for the other teams simply to act as *assemblatori* (constructors who assemble bought-in components). Serious teams must now have considerable manufacturing ability and access to high technology resources. Against a backdrop of increasing standards, improved annually by the most successful teams whose budgetary requirements are never static, even the smaller teams have had to move from the cottage industry approach towards manufacturing professionalism.

As aerodynamic advances continue, the top teams have their own wind tunnels and giant ovens (autoclaves) in which their carbon-fibre chassis are literally baked. Computer-assisted design equipment is essential, and as technology in that area improves, so costs rise further.

At races each team must operate like a small army, able to do battle in any conditions. Each needs at least one giant transporter which carries up to three racing cars and all the equipment necessary to make them competitive: spare engines and hundreds of spare parts. These are essential if the team's efforts are not to be compromised by any of the inevitable problems during the practice build-up to a race.

To the outsider the transporters may seem an extravagance, but they play a vital role

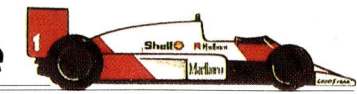

beyond merely taking the cars and spares from circuit to circuit. Once they are parked in the paddock they become the team's workshop, in conjunction with the pit garages. Any work required will be done either in the garage or in the transporter, away from prying eyes!

The transporters, and the motor-homes for entertaining VIP guests such as sponsors, are the visible evidence of how grand prix racing has progressed beyond the days when teams used to turn up at a race with their car towed on a trailer behind a small van. Now, thanks largely to the efforts of Bernard Ecclestone and the Formula One Constructors' Association (FOCA) since the early seventies, the rewards for teams have increased significantly in line with costs. Many more have thus been attracted to the sport's pinnacle. Not all are successful; some never will be, but others continue to progress and to challenge the established pacemakers. Grand prix racing has never been healthier.

Such is the interest in competing in grand prix racing that there are some 20 teams vying for grid positions in 1989. Besides those outlined below, Italian hopefuls are Osella, Minardi, Scuderia Italia and Coloni; Onyx joins the once-great British Tyrrell team, which aims to recapture past glory when it won championships with Jackie Stewart; and Euro Brun from Switzerland competes with AGS, the once successful Ligier *équipe* and Larrousse Calmels-Lola from France, and Rial and Zakspeed from West Germany. Some, like Tyrrell and Ligier, have shown in the past that they have what it takes to win races but most are on — and will be lucky to stay on — the lower rungs of a very slippery ladder.

Below Zakspeed typifies the small team in F1 — and the folly of going out on a limb with its own power source when proprietary units would have reaped better results.

Bottom Since Ron Dennis took control, McLaren International has been the dominant team of the Eighties.

11

Ferrari

Below *Ferrari tends to be either dominant or in the doldrums. Here at Long Beach in 1979 the 312 T4s of Villeneuve (12) and Scheckter lead Depailler's Ligier, Hunt's Wolf and Andretti's Lotus.*

Over the years Ferrari have won more grand prix races, (93), and constructors' championships (10) than any other team. They are the oldest team of them all, and the very name spells motor racing to the general public. The Italian team create a special atmosphere of their own wherever they go, as mechanics bustle round the scarlet racers in the pit lane before the drivers go out to tax them to the limit.

Many times the Latin temperament that is never far from the surface has frustrated smooth progress; Ferrari's history is one of turbulence. Successful periods have almost inevitably been followed by rapid declines. Jody Scheckter won the 1979 titles in the

312 T4, yet its replacement, the 312 T5, was a disaster. The first turbocharged 126CK was little better, yet the 126C2 brought the team back to the fore and, like its successor the 126C3, won the constructors' laurels. After another lull the F187 won the last two races of 1987 before being blown off comprehensively by McLaren and Honda throughout 1988.

Everyone loves the team, though, and urges them on to better things. Within F1 the unspoken belief is that a bad spell for Ferrari is a bad spell for the sport itself.

Enzo Ferrari's death in August 1988 raised a question mark over his company's future as part of the Fiat group, whose support he had solicited in 1968 when financial problems once again beset him. The future of this great team is thus uncertain. A lot depends on the success of John Barnard's latest design in the hands of Nigel Mansell and Gerhard Berger — and Mansell's storming Brazilian Grand Prix victory in the inaugural 1989 event was a huge (if unexpected) step in the right direction.

Above By 1988 Ferrari was playing second fiddle to McLaren, but the 1–2 scored by Berger and Alboreto at Monza was a poignant boost in the immediate wake of Enzo Ferrari's death.

Lotus

This British team is also one of the sport's older marques, with a glittering F1 history that dates back to 1958 and reflects the astonishing contribution made by its founder Colin Chapman.

A man of fertile imagination, Chapman introduced the monocoque chassis with his Lotus 25 in 1962. Brabham were the last team to stay with the old chassis-construction method of using tubular steel welded into a spaceframe. Everyone else followed Chapman's lead and switched to the markedly stiffer monocoque principle of construction.

With Ferrari and Brabham, Lotus were the first team to experiment with aerofoils in 1968, but perhaps Chapman's greatest legacy was to harness airflow beneath a car

Colin Chapman and Mario Andretti forged the same close relationship that had bonded the Lotus chief to Jim Clark. The championship eluded them in 1977, when they are seen with the Lotus 78 at Silverstone, but they made sure of it with the 79 the following year.

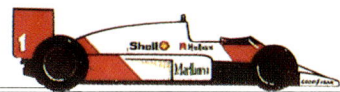

to increase its roadholding. In 1977 he introduced the Lotus 78 which was the forerunner of a new breed of grand prix cars. He followed it with the 79, which was even better. Mario Andretti and Ronnie Peterson dominated the 1978 season in the black and gold cars as everyone learned a new expression: 'ground effect'. Undaunted by the speed with which his major rivals caught on, and went on to beat him, Chapman began working on yet another ground-effect design, the Lotus 88, which was banned in 1981. He never quite recovered from that setback, and died suddenly in 1982, but his great team lives on.

Like Ferrari, Lotus have had their ups and downs. The eighties have not been as successful as the sixties and seventies, and though Ayrton Senna achieved 16 pole positions in his three years with the team, there were only eight wins to celebrate, split between him and the late Elio de Angelis. 1988, like 1980, 1981, 1983 and 1984, passed without major success, but after a dismal season Lotus are poised to bounce back in 1989.

Above Ayrton Senna was the saviour of Lotus during his years with the team. When John Player withdrew and Camel joined the team for 1987, he rewarded them with victory at Monaco – the first for a car with active suspension.

Controversy: the Lotus 88

The search for greater performance in the eighties spawned many intriguing mavericks, such as the Williams six-wheeler which used four small rear wheels to reduce frontal area and transmit the power more evenly. However, the most controversial was Colin Chapman's last great concept: the twin-chassised Lotus 88. The speed with which rivals caught up with his revolutionary 79, and the failure of his step-further 80, set Chapman seeking fresh avenues. The 88 provided them. It was two chassis in one car, the primary chassis carrying the bodywork, sidepods, aerofoils and radiators and the secondary, which fitted inside it, housing the engine, transmission, suspension, steering, braking, fuel tank and driver. The primary chassis was attached to the secondary by four coil spring/damper units mounted on to the bottom of the wheel uprights, which attach the wheels to the suspension.

Lotus claimed its aim was to isolate the driver from the pounding that had become part of a grand prix driver's role in the days of minimal suspension movement (something FISA had brought on F1 by banning sliding skirts). FISA, however, saw the primary chassis as a giant wing which acted directly on the wheel uprights (against the regulations) and after Lotus had tried unsuccessfully to race it four times, Chapman was finally forced to accept the ruling that his car was illegal. He was bitterly disappointed that another avenue of progress should be blocked, but as his anger subsided he began investigating active ride suspension instead.

THE TEAMS

McLaren

The class of '88: Ayrton Senna (12) and Alain Prost were unbeatable in their Honda-powered McLaren MP4/4s, seen here at the start of the Portuguese GP at Estoril. The Brazilian pipped the Frenchman to the world drivers' title.

McLaren have a shorter history than Ferrari and Lotus, but in the eighties are firmly established as one of the teams to beat. Of the nine constructors' championships since 1980, McLaren have won three, two of them consecutively, in 1984 and 1985. They have also won four drivers' titles: one for Niki Lauda, two for Alain Prost and one for Ayrton Senna.

Bruce McLaren formed his own F1 team for the 1966 season, having raced sports cars bearing his name before that. By 1968 his cars were winning races and his team-mate Denny Hulme was a contender for the championship. After McLaren was killed testing a new sports car in 1970, co-director Teddy Mayer carried on, and the team won the drivers' and constructors' championships with Emerson Fittipaldi in 1974 and the drivers' again with James Hunt in 1976.

After that McLaren fortunes waned, and in 1981 an uneasy partnership was forged with a promising Formula Two team owner called Ron Dennis, who had already commissioned John Barnard to design him a grand prix car. That became the McLaren

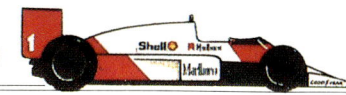

MP4/1, which signalled a revolution in chassis-construction techniques, and ushered in a highly successful range of racing cars.

Mayer and the old guard eventually parted company with the team, leaving Dennis in sole charge. Barnard left in 1986 but, far from stumbling, McLaren moved from strength to strength as Dennis' carefully formed corporate structure began to show its true worth. With a modified car Alain Prost won the 1986 drivers' championship.

Against Williams he was unable to compete on sheer horsepower in 1987, when the Honda V6 was just too strong for the TAG Porsche V6, but in 1988 McLaren too had Honda power and dominated the season; but for an incident with a slower driver at Monza, they might well have won all 16 races. As it was Ayrton Senna won the drivers' championship from team-mate Prost, and McLaren were a massive 134 points ahead of Ferrari in the constructors'. Their final tally of 199 was only two points short of the total of all the other teams put together, and by any standards it was an overwhelming success that underlined how effectively Dennis has spent his multi-million pound budget.

Back in 1979 things had not been so rosy for the team. Here at Silverstone for the British GP John Watson struggles with the M29, which had just replaced the unsuccessful M28.

Williams

In 1986/87 the Williams–Hondas were the fastest cars in F1, but team-mates Nigel Mansell and Nelson Piquet, seen here fighting for the 1987 French GP at Paul Ricard, seldom evinced feelings of camaraderie.

Williams are another team of much the same vintage, and also a major force in the late 1980s. Williams won four constructors' championship, and also won the world drivers' championships for Alan Jones, Keke Rosberg and Nelson Piquet.

Williams graduated to F1 in 1969, three years after McLaren, when Frank Williams bought a Brabham BT26, installed a Cosworth engine, and hired his friend Piers Courage to drive it. The result was a brilliant pair of second places that seemed to set the team on course for greatness. That greatness did eventually come – but not for another 10 years.

In 1970 Williams did a deal to run De Tomaso's new car, but when Courage was killed in it in the Dutch GP, the team's fortunes went into a downward spiral. For years they struggled on, as Frank frantically pulled deals together in time to go racing each season. Rarely did the same spark shine through, however. His team was acquired by another; but in 1977 he secured financial support from Saudi Arabia, and set up on his own again with the gifted designer Patrick Head.

In 1978 they emerged as the only Cosworth team fully able to compete with Lotus, and in 1979 Head's brilliant FW07 design finally put Williams on the map as Clay Regazzoni won the team's first victory in the British GP and Alan Jones was unlucky to miss out on the world title to Jody Scheckter. He won the following season, and since then Williams have been a truly front-running team.

They were the last to take a title with Cosworth power, when Rosberg cannily beat the increasingly threatening turbos in the

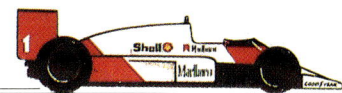

1982 world drivers' championship, and the first to make Honda's V6 a race-winner in 1984. Between the end of 1985 and the end of the 1987 season they were the class of the field as Nigel Mansell won 13 GPs, Nelson Piquet seven and Keke Rosberg two.

McLaren's incredible 1988 season put the then Judd-powered Williams team in the shade, although Nigel Mansell hounded Ayrton Senna and Alain Prost in three races; but with Renault's new V10 the team are determined to take on the McLaren-Hondas on even terms in 1989.

Alan Jones, heading for victory in Canada in his 1980 World Championship year, was the perfect driver for Patrick Head's brilliantly successful ground-effect Williams FW07.

Renault

The team which introduced the turbocharger to grand prix racing in 1979 seemed on the verge of major success time and again after their maiden win in 1977, but somehow it never materialised despite a massive budget.

Each year they produced a new car, and improved its trail-blazing V6 engine to produce yet more power; yet each time Alain Prost drew a bead on the world championship, something went wrong. In 1981 they took too long to get their RE30 working properly after the rules had been changed. In 1982 their reliability record was lamentable: Prost or René Arnoux dominated seven races, only to retire. In 1983 Prost had an excellent chance of the title in the sleek RE40 but reliability, and a rare driving error at Zandvoort, conspired against him and cost Renault their last realistic opportunity. The works team stayed in racing for another

two seasons, pairing Derek Warwick and Patrick Tambay, but they were a shadow of their former selves and eventually corporate embarrassment led to a decision to quit.

Motor racing, especially at Grand Prix level, is often all about personalities rather than machinery. Exciting though the latter undoubtedly is, it needs those personalities to make it live. At Renault everything was done by committee. The vital spark that a personality such as Ron Dennis's or Frank Williams's can ignite was never present to start with, and the whole saga became an object lesson to other major manufacturers. Those with little experience of racing would do far better to place their future prospects in the hands of a team that does know what to do. Honda proved this conclusively with its associations with Williams and McLaren, and to a lesser degree with Lotus. BMW did so, too, with Brabham.

By 1982 Renault had ironed out most of the faults of its innovative turbocharged car. Here Alain Prost leads René Arnoux in the South African Grand Prix that year.

Above *Back in 1977, however, when the turbo made its debut at Silverstone, it was met with scepticism and even ridicule.*

Brabham

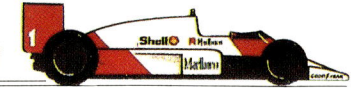

Like McLaren named after a highly successful grand prix driver, Brabham have undergone several significant character changes since they were bought by Bernard Ecclestone in 1971. Throughout the seventies their cars, designed by Gordon Murray, were innovative and original, and the South African carried that trait through into the eighties. His 1979 BT48 design had been hampered by under-powered Alfa Romeo V12 engines, but it moved into 1980 as the Cosworth-propelled BT49 and proved a match for the dominant Williams FW07 as Nelson Piquet's talent blossomed.

Murray and Piquet formed a strong alliance that led to narrow defeat in the 1980 title chase and victory the following season, and after a hiatus in 1982 as they developed the package of the BT50 and the turbocharged BMW engine, they bounced back in 1983 for another championship.

Murray's BT52 was typically different, with pointed nose, short sidepods and rearward weight bias like a dragster, and its BT53 and BT54 successors proved to be among the elite capable of challenging the all-conquering McLaren TAG-Porsches in 1984 and 1985. The subsequent BT55, however, indicated just how easy it is for a designer to be lured down a blind alley. Murray produced a very low-line car with the BMW engine inclined to reduce frontal area, but the laydown version of the four-cylinder turbo never produced the same power as its upright predecessor, and the schedule of a hectic season did not allow the team time to develop their new package.

Thus in one short year Brabham fell from grace, Murray left to join McLaren after becoming disenchanted, and the once-great team never recaptured the lost glory with the BT54-derived BT56 of 1987. They sat out 1988, but returned under new ownership and with most of the existing personnel in 1989. Whether Brabham regains their front-running place remains to be seen.

Left Ever the innovator, Brabham designer Gordon Murray helped Nelson Piquet to his first World Championship with the hydraulic suspension set-up he produced to bypass the 1981 ground-clearance regulations. Here winner Piquet heads for the pits with the car in raised state during qualifying for the Argentinian GP.

Below Never afraid to experiment. Murray penned the lowline BT55 for 1985, but lack of development and engine problems rendered it an also-ran.

Benetton

When sponsor Benetton bought Toleman for the 1986 season, it invested in a team that had shown great promise after a shaky start. As a Formula Two team in 1980 Toleman had swept all before it to win the European championship, and embarked ambitiously on an F1 programme with the Hart turbocharged four-cylinder engine. Designer Rory Byrne's TG181 proved overweight and struggled to qualify everywhere in 1981 as they battled to learn the ropes. It was massaged into a mid-field runner the following year, and in 1983 its successor, the TG183, finally began to suggest that the team had a future.

In the years up to their purchase by the Italian clothing group Byrne's TG184 and TG185 designs earned a reputation for handling excellence. They nearly scored their first win at Monaco in 1984 when Ayrton Senna was closing on Alain Prost in the rain, but the race was stopped prematurely. In 1986 the overdue maiden triumph finally did come—for Gerhard Berger in Mexico in the BMW-powered B186; and since then Benetton have worked hard to build reliability and speed into their cars. From a pit lane joke in 1981, the team have polished themselves into one of the most respected contenders.

Above *Since it bought out Toleman, the Benetton Group's Rory Byrne-designed cars have earned a reputation for fine handling. Here Thierry Boutsen checks practice lap times with assistant team manager Gordon Message.*

Left Gerhard Berger scored his and Benetton's first F1 victory in Mexico in 1986.

Above Cut-away drawing of Byrne's Benetton B187.

Left Boutsen leads Gerhard Berger (Ferrari) and Nigel Mansell (Williams) in the 1987 Austrian GP.

Arrows

Victory has eluded Arrows International so far, but at Monza in 1988 Eddie Cheever drove the Ross Brawn A10B design to one of its best placings, with third spot behind the Ferraris of Berger and Alboreto.

This team, however, still await that breakthrough victory, despite the fact that their first car, the FA1, led in only its second race, in South Africa in 1978. Since then founders Jack Oliver and Alan Rees have shown that endurance is every bit as essential as sheer financial wherewithal, but Arrows International remain one of the longest-established outfits never to have won a grand prix. Indeed, since those early days they have rarely looked likely to, Thierry Boutsen's second in an A8 at Imola in 1985 and Eddie Cheever's third in an A10B at Monza in 1988 being their closest. But since designer Ross Brawn joined in 1987, there has been a new purpose within the team.

March

Like McLaren and Williams they are a long established team, set up in 1970 by Robin Herd, Max Mosley, Graham Coaker and Alan Rees. They burst on to the grand prix scene boasting drivers of the calibre of Jackie Stewart, Chris Amon and Mario Andretti in the cockpits of their 701s. Stewart won the Spanish GP and Amon the International Trophy at Silverstone that year, but it was another five years before Vittorio Brambilla won in Austria in a 751. March's story was always the same: Herd would concentrate on the Formula Two and Formula Three cars which earned the bread and butter, and only infrequently was there enough money to race properly in Formula One.

Early in the eighties he toyed with it again with the 811 and the 821, but neither was competitive and he finally pulled out, vowing not to return until he could do so properly. In 1986, however, he hatched plans with Akira Akagi, the head of the giant Japanese Leyton House property business, and after a learning year in 1987 former journalist Ian Phillips headed a team that rocked the 1988 establishment by hounding

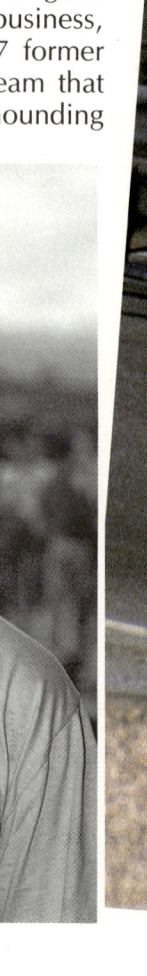

Right Adrian Newey brought some CART racing aerodynamic thinking to F1 with his striking March 881 (**main picture**) which often showed itself to be the quickest of the non-turbo cars in 1988.

McLarens in Portugal and actually leading them – for a glorious 400 yards – in Japan. On several occasions the Adrian Newey-designed 881s proved the fastest normally-aspirated challengers, ahead of the Williams FW12s and the Benetton B188s. To the equation that makes up a successful grand prix team was restored enjoyment, once an essential but which had been lost as commercialism swept through F1. Phillips' down-to-earth crew thoroughly enjoyed their racing, acting as a close-knit unit whose two hungry young drivers, Ivan Capelli and Mauricio Gugelmin, were frequently to be seen performing chauffeur duties in the team's bus.

The Team Chiefs

arlboro
NACIONAL
Shell
BOSS
Marlboro

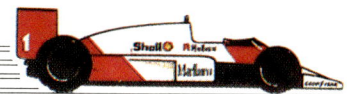

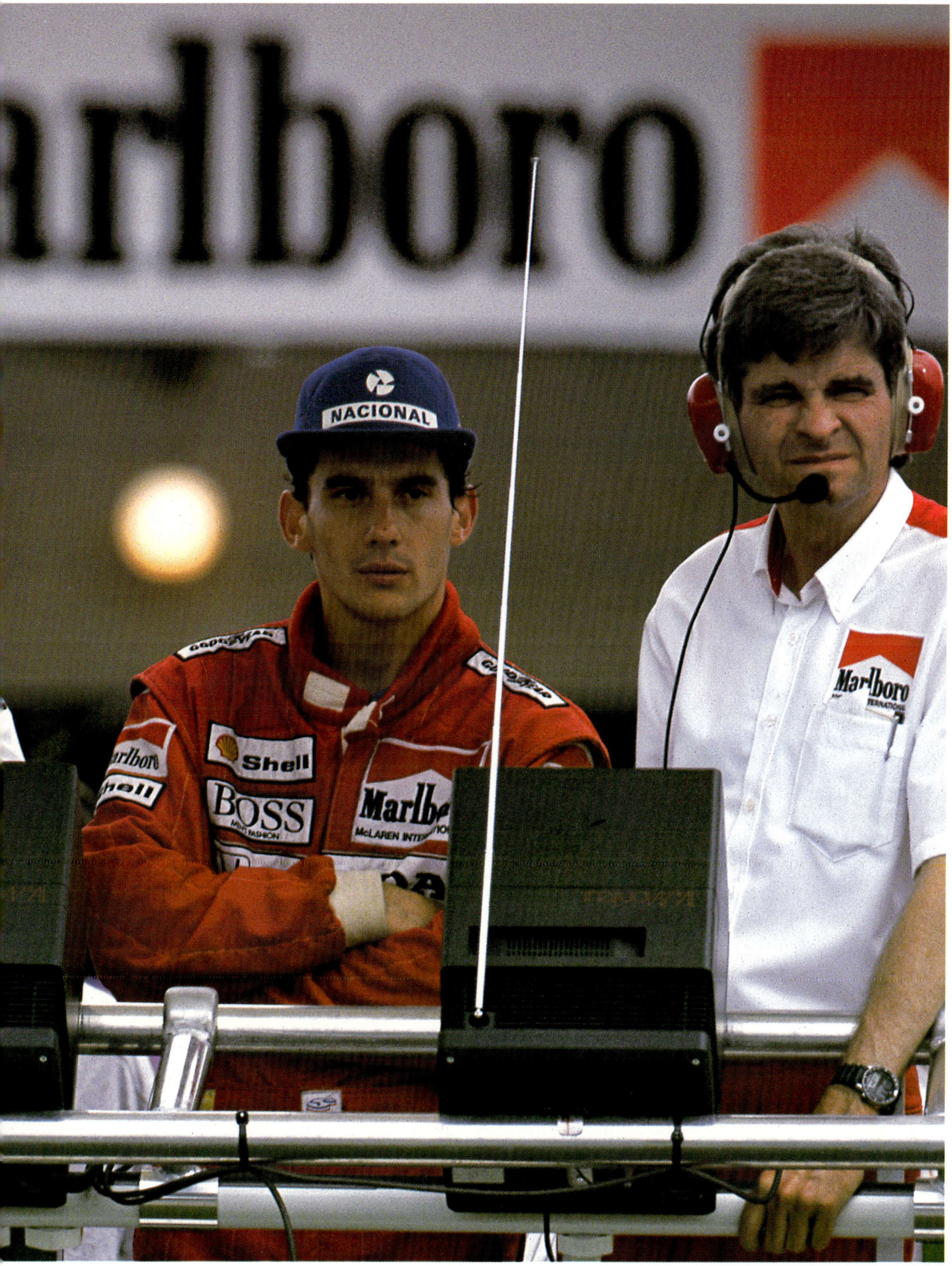

Enzo Ferrari

Above Enzo Ferrari was the charismatic, autocratic founder and prime mover of the greatest dynasty of racing machines until his death, aged 90, in 1988.

Preceding two pages
Organiser extraordinaire: Ron Dennis proved himself the manager of the Eighties as he built McLaren International to superteam status. Here (left to right) Gordon Murray, Dennis, Ayrton Senna and designer Steve Nichols monitor Prost's winning progress after Senna had been disqualified from the 1988 Brazilian GP.

Enzo Ferrari could be cunning, irascible and cruel. To some of his employees he was a dictator who ruled his domain in Maranello with a rod of iron and liked to leave his drivers dangling like rejected puppets. At times, however, he was a sympathetic father figure who simply believed that making everyone competitive with one another was the best way to bring out their latent abilities. Beneath it all he was a true racer, with a racer's instincts honed during his own successful career behind the steering wheel.

Born in February 1898, he took to motor sport early and, after a moderately successful career as a driver, set up his own Scuderia Ferrari in 1929, running factory Alfa Romeos for the likes of Tazio Nuvolari until 1938, when Alfa took the operation back under their own wing. Never one to accept another's authority, Ferrari left and set up his own company – and thus was a legend born.

Throughout the fifties and sixties Ferraris came to epitomise the romance of motor racing, Ferrari's own rather mysterious personal behaviour – he rarely attended races – adding to the legend. In the seventies his red cars won four constructors' and three drivers' titles, and though the eighties were

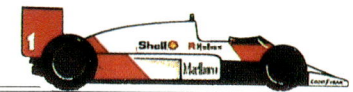

less successful, Ferraris still won the constructors' championship in 1982 and 1983. By the time of his death on 14 August 1988 they had won 92 grand prix and nine Le Mans races. When Ayrton Senna's McLaren spun on to the Monza kerbing in September, and the Ferraris of Gerhard Berger and Michele Alboreto stormed home to their first

1-2 at the track since 1979, the *tifosi* (the excitable supporters of the Prancing Horse) went wild. Enzo Ferrari was no longer there to watch the success on television at home, savouring a post-prandial whisky; but his cars could still excite the emotions of a nation. And as long as there is motor racing, they always will.

Didier Pironi in the Ferrari 126CK – the Prancing Horse's first turbo car – during the 1981 Monaco Grand Prix.

Colin Chapman

Anthony Colin Bruce Chapman was a bright-eyed, far-seeing visionary who built racing and road cars in the Ferrari tradition and was never afraid to try anything. He was a concept man capable of quite remarkable lateral thinking, who was also astute enough to listen to his engineers and try their ideas.

It was he who introduced the monocoque chassis and inclined driving position to F1 with the 1962 Lotus 25, which was refined into the hyper-successful 33. It was he who rewrote the design parameters with the 49, the Maurice Philipe-designed car which was the first to carry the now legendary Ford Cosworth DFV engine. Two years later Chapman also experimented with four-wheel drive, before introducing the wedge shape with Philipe's 72 in 1970.

Few designers ever matched the late Colin Chapman's brilliant flair for lateral thinking and innovation as he built Lotus into one of motor racing's most respected teams.

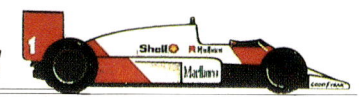

Perhaps his greatest contribution as a manufacturer of light, fast race winners was harnessing ground effect, with the 78 in 1977 and the championship-winning 79 the following year.

The 80 typified Chapman's way of thinking: he could simply have revised the 79s for another year but, instead, pressed further with the 80, which simply didn't work as well. But Chapman reasoned that they learned valuable lessons from it. Later, in 1981, he produced the twin-chassis 88 which sought to have its ground effect cake and eat it, while giving the drivers a more comfortable ride. He lost a little of his enthusiasm when FISA banned it, but it was rekindled as Elio de Angelis beat Keke Rosberg to the line by a scant 0.05 of a second in the 1982 Austrian Grand Prix in his 91. Chapman, as usual, threw his cap high into the air in celebration, no doubt recalling his maxim 'If you're not winning, you're not trying'. Only months later he was dead, killed by a heart attack. Like Ferrari, however, the astonishing legend of Chapman and his cars lives on.

After Chapman's sadly early death in 1982, Ayrton Senna kept Lotus's flag flying. Here he leads Nigel Mansell in his win at Jerez in 1986.

35

Bernie Ecclestone

Shrewd, calculating and far-sighted, Bernie Ecclestone fought the war with FISA on FOCA's behalf and was the archiect of modern F1, while simultaneously giving designer Gordon Murray a free rein to produce race-winning Brabhams.

Beneath his sometimes gruff exterior, highly successful businessman Ecclestone is a racer. He was an accomplished performer in the old 500cc Formula Three days before managing Vanwall star Stuart Lewis-Evans,

Bernie Ecclestone isn't famous because of the racing cars he builds — although between 1971 and 1988 he did own the Brabham team, which added two drivers' championships to the tally they had garnered during Sir Jack's ownership in the 1960s. Rather, Ecclestone's contribution to motor racing history is to have dragged the sport into the commercial era, and to have shaped it into the multi-million pound industry that it now is.

The lower levels of the sport take their lead from grand prix racing, and as Ecclestone made improvements in F1, the same developments have filtered down. He began by forming the Formula One Constructors' Association (FOCA) to give the competing teams a common voice. Gradually he improved their image, created a recognised prize fund and one with preferential travel rates for successful teams, and organised and promoted races abroad to give F1 the right image as a world-wide sport. Over the years he also revolutionised television coverage to the point where grand prix racing is now seen by millions around the globe.

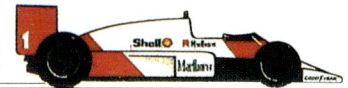

and he was astute enough to give designer Gordon Murray free rein at Brabham without cramping his style.

In a fast-moving sport he was also the one team owner who took time to look after everyone's interests, and was the principal opponent of the governing body during the acrimonious FISA/FOCA war in 1980. FISA (Fédération International de Sport Automobile) wanted to ban aerodynamic sliding skirts overnight, and to run the financial side of F1 as well as making the rules. FOCA felt the ban would load the dice too heavily in favour of the turbocharged cars from the major manufacturers such as Renault and Ferrari, and weren't prepared to surrender the financial ground they had won by persistent effort. In 1981 Ecclestone eventually hammered out the Concorde Agreement by which all teams are still bound, effectively creating the backdrop against which GP racing is now run, and the financial structure from which all the successful teams benefit. In 1988 he sold his interest in Brabham, having taken over as vice-president of marketing in FISA.

Gordon Murray's Brabham BT49 brought Nelson Piquet his first drivers' title in 1981.

Frank Williams

Above Frank Williams built Williams from a hand-to-mouth team to one of F1's major protagonists through a blend of aggression, excellent design and sheer determination – the latter undiminished by the 1986 accident which left him paralysed.

Right Keke Rosberg in the 1983 Williams–Ford FW08 confers with team members during qualifying.

When Frank Williams entered the press tent at the 1986 British Grand Prix everyone stood and applauded loudly, an emotional indication of the regard in which Williams Grand Prix Engineering's boss is held by the world's motor-racing fraternity.

Six months earlier he had been paralysed from the waist down in a car accident in the south of France, hours after watching a test session at the Paul Ricard circuit which confirmed designer Patrick Head's new FW11 as highly competitive. The accident was a cruel blow to a man to whom physical fitness had played an essential role as he built up his team, but it was not enough to stem his unquenchable enthusiasm for motor racing.

He started by trading in second-hand cars as he scratched together enough money to race himself. He was fast, but his cars frequently suffered. When he became an entrant his fortunes improved, and if Piers Courage had not been killed at Zandvoort in 1970 driving the Williams-entered De Tomaso, the success Williams finally achieved in the eighties would probably have come much sooner. Instead, he struggled on and at one stage his team were taken over by Austro-Canadian oil magnate Walter Wolf. Williams later departed to set up on his own again and this time, with Head designing, he was much more successful. By 1979 his team had won their first grand prix and since then have never looked back. With Head, Williams perfected the second-generation ground effect racer, and together they created the structure on which Alan Jones, Keke Rosberg and Nelson Piquet won world championships. It is a tribute to his team's strength that Piquet succeeded in the year Frank himself had his accident. After years of toil and tragedy, he now takes his rightful place as a cornerstone of British motor racing history.

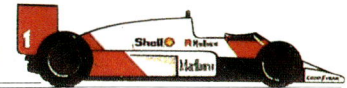

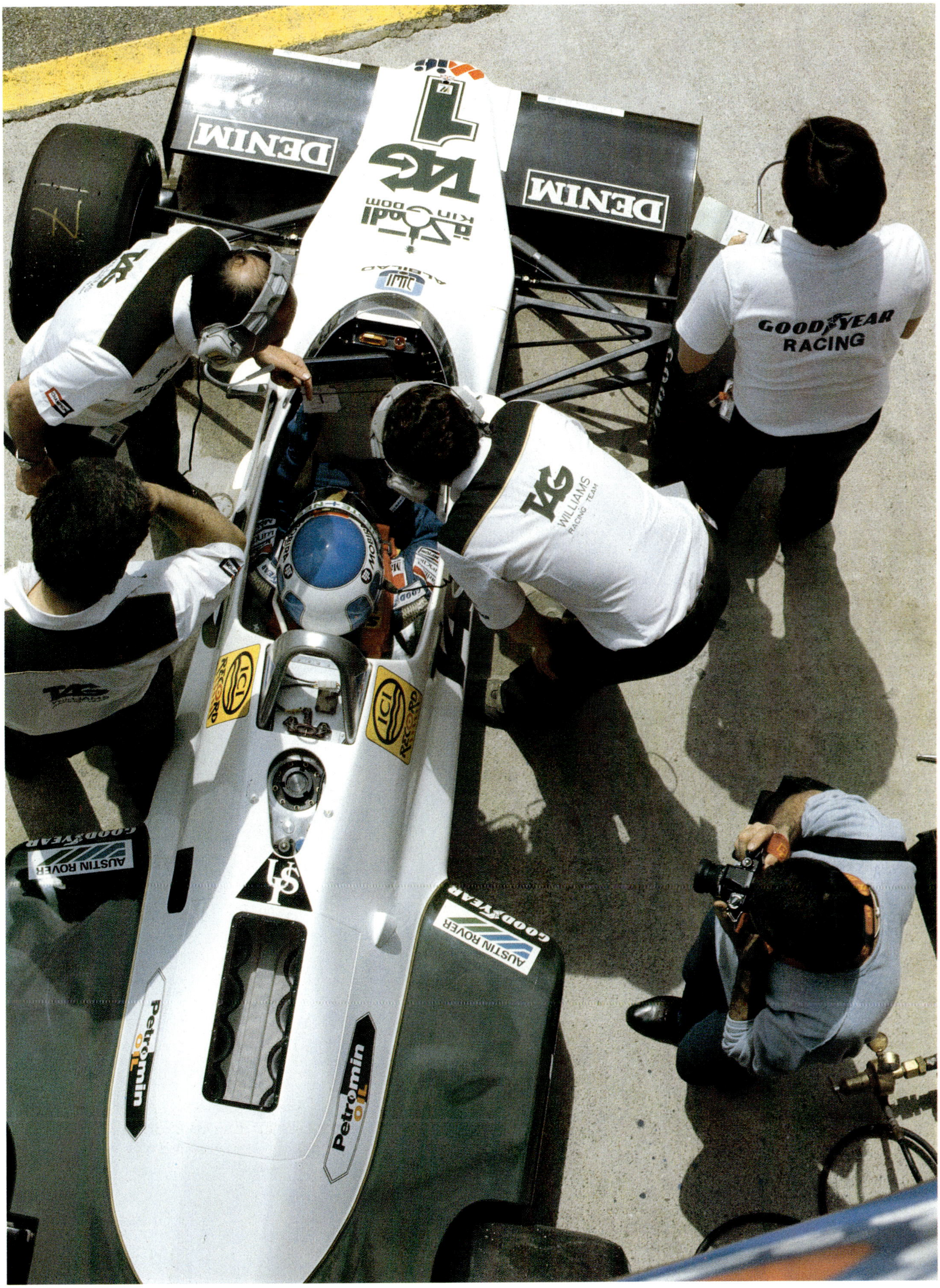
DENIM
DENIM
TAG
GOODYEAR
RACING
TAG
WILLIAMS
RACING TEAM
AUSTIN ROVER
GOODYEAR
Petromin
OIL
Petromin
OIL

Ron Dennis

Ron Dennis brought to F1 the organisational flair that had won him an F3 championship and numerous F2 successes.

Ron Dennis is the architect of the mega-dollar budget in modern grand prix racing, and the owner of the most successful team in recent history. A former mechanic for Cooper and Brabham (where he worked on Sir Jack's car), he struck out on his own, set up his team and progressed through Formula Three and Formula Two to his goal of F1. He already had John Barnard working on a new F1 design when he engineered a merger between his own Project Four company and McLaren, to form McLaren International. When Barnard's new car, the first full carbon-fibre design, which became the

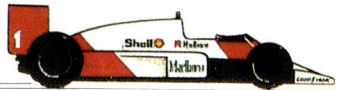

McLaren MP4/1, won the 1981 British Grand Prix and was highly competitive elsewhere, it was obvious that the impressive newcomers had a car and the team to ensure a bright future.

Dennis's ability to source finance was one of the factors which opened the way to the explosion of high technology within F1. Now McLaren manufacture virtually everything on their cars bar the Honda engines and the Goodyear tyres. Their successes are an enduring endorsement for McLaren's and other sponsors of the value of motorsport as a marketing promotion – so long as you pick a team capable of creating winners!

Dennis's relationship with Alain Prost – here clinching his second title at Adelaide in 1986 – was a big factor in McLaren's success story.

Ken Tyrrell

*Ken Tyrrell, a top contender in the days of Jackie Stewart, is a true survivor. Through the good times and bad he has kept Tyrrell afloat, and in 1987 Jonathan Palmer (**main picture**) rewarded his persistence with success in the Jim Clark and Colin Chapman championships for normally aspirated cars.*

Ken Tyrrell was winning world championships when Dennis was still wielding spanners, and though their respective circumstances have changed over the years, he remains an illuminating example of how to keep going in a tough world even though one's greatest successes lie far behind.

As a driver Tyrrell was successful in the 500cc Formula Three, but it was as an entrant that he was destined to make his mark. In the early sixties the timber merchant from Surrey built a fearsome reputation as he entered Jackie Stewart in Formula Three and Jacky Ickx in Formula Two, with sensational success. By 1968 he had graduated to F1 with Stewart and Matra, and by 1969 they were champions of the world.

When Matra withdrew in 1970 Tyrrell bought a March and initiated secret con-

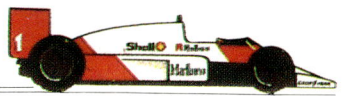

struction of his own car, which appeared later in the year to the amazement of the specialist press. In 1971 and 1973 Stewart again won titles for the team. Tyrrell's ability to keep a secret was never better illustrated than when he launched his P34 in 1975. Nobody knew it had six wheels until the dustsheets were lifted.

Since their last grand prix win at Detroit in 1983 the team has struggled to live up to their illustrious past. In 1984 motor racing's governing body, FISA, accused Tyrrell of cheating and took away all his points won that year, but he vehemently protested his innocence, fought back and was vindicated.

Design Developments

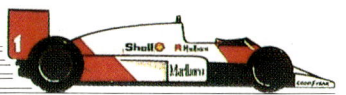

THE TEAMS

Chassis

Preceding two pages The modern F1 chassis laid bare, courtesy of McLaren. The composite fuselage, large central fuel tank and compact engine/transmission package had become universal by 1988, but the fuel began to spread again around the driver's hips on some designs as the new footbox regulations came into force.

Below left In 1962 Colin Chapman's Lotus 25 revolutionised chassis design with its monocoque structure, and set a style that was to be followed universally in Formula 1.

Below right Harvey Postlethwaite's 1979 Wolf WR8, driven here by James Hunt at Long Beach, was one of the first F1 cars to feature a chassis formed fully in honeycomb aluminium.

The chassis is the heart of the modern grand prix car. Of course, other major areas such as the engine, transmission, suspension and driver must also be up to the job, but if the basic chassis isn't right, nothing else can compensate.

The Lotus 100T illustrated the point nicely in 1988. It had a world champion driver (Nelson Piquet) and the same turbocharged Honda V6 engine and Goodyear tyres as the McLaren MP4/4; but whereas the McLarens won 15 of the 16 world championship races, the Lotus never looked remotely like winning one, and its best results were two third places. The difference was mainly in the chassis and no matter how much the team modified its suspension geometry and the aerodynamics, the car remained unable to compete on even terms with its supposedly similar rival.

During the eighties grand prix chassis construction techniques developed dramatically, in a way they hadn't since Colin Chapman built the first successful monocoque Lotus 25 in 1962. Towards the end of the seventies designers had been feeling their way with carbon-fibre and Kevlar composites which had been developed in the USA and Britain for the aircraft industry, and were now available to other areas. Ground effect was well established, and chassis designers began to seek new methods of stiffening their structures as the loads being fed into the monocoques were now so enormous. As an example Patrick Head, designer for Williams, had to engineer twice the stiffness into the FW07, his first ground effect car, than he did into the conventional FW06 which the team had run the previous year. No matter how good the car's aerodynamics were, it had to have a torsionally rigid chassis to optimise its undercar downforce.

1980 was a year of consolidation, with carbon-fibre limited to stiffening panels in non-stress-bearing areas of the chassis, wings, and brake discs. Gordon Murray, for example, had for some time used panels to stiffen his Brabhams, and did so again on the BT49. Honeycomb composites were not new: in 1966 Bruce McLaren's first F1 car, the M2B, was built in Mallite, thin aluminium sheeting which sandwiched a balsa wood honeycomb and came from the aircraft industry; in the same year Ford ran their Le Mans J car, which was built in aluminium honeycomb and became the highly successful MkIV in 1967; two years after that Cooper built a T90 F5000 monocoque in aluminium honeycomb sandwiched between an outer skin of aluminium and an inner skin of glass-reinforced plastic; in the seventies McLaren had aluminium honeycomb in their M26; and Harvey Postlethwaite used it for his Wolf WR8 chassis in 1979. By the beginning of the eighties they still weren't widespread, however, but more

F1 designers were beginning to use honeycomb aluminium in their chassis for structural rigidity. Much research went into the optimum adhesive for bond strength and longevity, but opinion was still divided on impact resistance, some still favouring standard sheet aluminium.

As the debate continued, John Barnard was turning his thoughts to a composite chassis for the new car he was drawing for Ron Dennis. The outcome was to revolutionise grand prix racing. What became the McLaren MP4/1 when Project 4 and McLaren were pushed into amalgamation by sponsor Marlboro was the first carbon-

What are composites?

More than anything, the Eighties will be remembered as the decade in which composite materials became mandatory for grand prix car construction. But what are composites?

In the engineering sense, they are an amalgam of materials, such as fibreglass and polyester resin, or aluminium panels which sandwich an aluminium or balsa wood honeycomb. To the grand prix enthusiast composites mean mixtures of carbon-fibre and Kevlar mats, bonded together with advanced adhesives such as phenolic resin which requires heat curing before it sets fully.

fibre composite F1 chassis, a major departure from the accepted norm. When it won the British GP in 1981 – and then withstood a major accident later that season in the Italian GP at Monza – Barnard's adventurous gamble was totally vindicated. Apart from carbon-fibre's tremendous strength, its major advantage was its low weight compared with aluminium, and the fact that far fewer parts were needed to make a monocoque, saving even more.

At the same time that Barnard was designing the MP4/1 Chapman and Peter Wright were also working on the carbon-fibre Lotus 88 chassis. However, whereas Barnard opted for some complex shapes, Lotus used flat carbon-fibre panels bonded together to form a relatively simple structure.

After the carbon-fibre breakthrough the next significant landmark was the addition of Kevlar. Carbon-fibre itself is relatively brittle, but inner layers of the even lighter

Above At the beginning of the Eighties, John Barnard's McLaren MP4/1 brought the next great revolution. Its carbon-fibre chassis was initially greeted with scepticism; within years all F1 cars used composites.

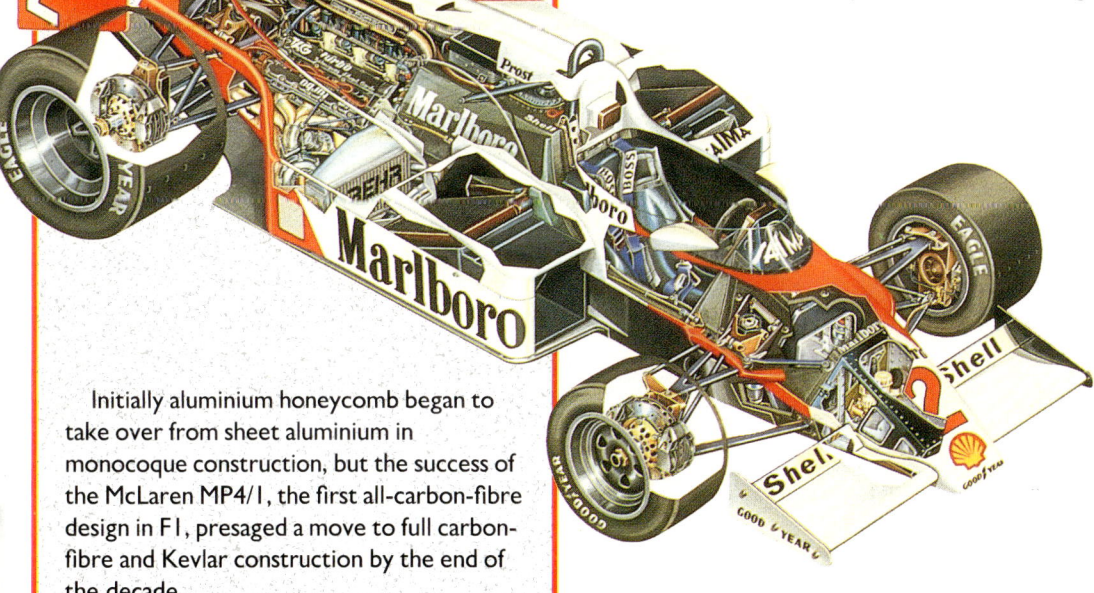

Initially aluminium honeycomb began to take over from sheet aluminium in monocoque construction, but the success of the McLaren MP4/1, the first all-carbon-fibre design in F1, presaged a move to full carbon-fibre and Kevlar construction by the end of the decade.

Above Manfred Winkelhock in the ATS D6, the first car to use a full composite 'tub' that also acted as the outer bodywork.

Below Ferrari's 1981 126CK had a reputation for unpredictable handling.

and cheaper Kevlar mat provided greater resistance to tearing and even more strength. Other materials such as Nomex reduced fire risk, too. As more designers came to appreciate yet another virtue, the incredible stiffness of carbon-fibre/Kevlar monocoques, so the movement away from aluminium structures increased.

In 1983 came a further step. Barnard had opted for a self-contained 'bathtub' chassis structure with separate bodywork, but the Austrian designer Gustav Brunner penned the neat D6 chassis for ATS in which the upper section of the monocoque above the driver's legs also formed the upper bodywork, so that the very stiff tub required only a small composite nose section.

Both Ferrari and Williams, renowned for their cautious approaches, remained faithful to the aluminium monocoque longer than most of their rivals. At the start of the eighties Ferrari persisted with their long-held philosophy that the engine was the heart of the car, and the chassis of secondary importance. Their 1981 126CK epitomised this approach, harnessing its plentiful turbo power in an unruly chassis consisting essentially of a spaceframe with a riveted aluminium skin. That gave way the following year to the stop-gap 126C2, a markedly better car that earned an unjustified reputation for weakness in the wake of Gilles Villeneuve's fatal accident at Zolder in 1982 and his team-mate Didier Pironi's later on at Hockenheim. Only in mid-1983 was designer Harvey Postlethwaite's new carbon-fibre 126C3 ready, and it utilised the same approach as Brunner's ATS.

The 1985 Williams FW10 was Patrick Head's first all-carbon-fibre chassis, both the FW08 and FW09 making use of alumin-

ium honeycomb tubs with progressively more carbon-fibre components such as body panels and wings. One of the principal reasons for Williams taking so much longer was Head's reluctance to switch construction methods until the team had sufficient experience to do their own work in-house. Predictably, when he felt the time had come, he got it right first time.

As cars' power increased with the development of the turbocharged grand prix engine, chassis became stiffer and stiffer to cope with the extra horsepower and the increased cornering loads fed into them. Racing also became very much safer. Before John Watson's accident in the McLaren MP4/1 at Monza sceptics had predicted that carbon-fibre chassis would shatter after the first serious impact. That proved incorrect, and FISA strengthened its safety rules for 1982 by requiring a protective structure around the driver's feet. These were updated over the years to the point where each design's nosebox must undergo a successful crash test before the car can race. Few who witnessed Nelson Piquet's accident at Imola in 1987, Philipe Alliot's in Mexico or Derek Warwick's in Montreal in 1988, doubted that they would have been very badly injured if they had not been in carbon-fibre/Kevlar chassis. Instead, all

three escaped dazed but otherwise unharmed from accidents that would have been fatal in the sixties and seventies. To protect drivers further, FISA decreed that their feet were to be behind the front axle centre-line in all new 1988 chassis and allowed only existing, updated chassis to site them ahead. For 1989 all cars must conform to the new regulations.

Aerodynamics

Alongside the giant strides in chassis construction went significant further progress on the aerodynamic front, if not in quite such quantum leaps as ground effect had triggered.

FISA banned shaped undersides and skirts in November 1982 and insisted that the area between the rear edge of a car's front tyres and the front edge of its rears should be absolutely flat. Only in the area behind the leading edge of the rear tyres could the underbody still flick up to form a diffusor. Cars still run to these regulations, and still produce a measure of ground effect, but at that stage designers were faced with a loss of some 60 per cent of the downforce they had become used to, at a time when power outputs were nudging up to the 650bhp mark. The larger wings created more drag, but there was more power to overcome it, so the equation balanced and began to tip in favour of faster lap times than the old ground effect racers' as the horsepower race continued.

Little nuances crept in. The front wings began to grow small side skirts to create their own venturi effect, and several designers experimented with the sort of scalloped front wings that Rory Byrne introduced on the Toleman TG184. Further back, rear wings began to sprout ugly little winglets outside their endplates, until FISA banned them for 1985.

The most successful way of retrieving some of the lost downforce was Barnard's idea of sweeping in the bodywork just ahead of the rear wheels, like a Coca Cola bottle shape, to lead on to upturned ramps mounted inboard of each rear wheel. It was widely copied within weeks.

The 1984 McLaren–TAG MP4/2 followed the aerodynamic fashion by using small extension winglets ahead of the rear axle line, and set a trend of its own with its pronounced 'coke-bottle' waisting of the rear bodywork.

How ground effect works

When a racing car is travelling at speed, air passes over, around and underneath it. Until 1977 most aerodynamic work centred on shaping and controlling the airflow over and around it, but after that time the flow beneath it became critical.

If a car runs low to the ground, the air beneath it is constricted as it passes through the narrow gap. According to the scientist Daniel Bernoulli's theory, when airflow is restricted through a venturi (a narrow opening that becomes progressively wider), it speeds up but its pressure is reduced. Thus, in a racing car, as the air flows faster through the venturis shaped into its lower bodywork, its pressure becomes lower than that of the air acting over the top of the car and the car is hugged to the ground by the suction effect created. This in turn creates higher loadings on the tyres, and significantly increases cornering force.

The original ground effect cars used carefully shaped venturis beneath the box-shaped 'sidepods' between their wheels, and the underside of the car swept gently upwards behind the rear axle to form a

Otherwise the search for the elusive perfect aerodynamic form became a matter of minute refinement, and as minimal frontal area became a priority again, the very shape of the monocoque was to be influenced by wind-cheating requirements. In the ground effect days chassis had been made as slim as possible to maximise sidepod area, and that aim still holds today as designers seek to present the smallest area of car to the wind. Byrne pioneered the super-narrow nose on his Benetton B187, whose monocoque bulged out behind the nosebox. March's Adrian Newey took the approach a step further by making his 881 tub so super-narrow that its drivers could barely squeeze in and added a nuance of his own, a step beneath the pointed nose to create further downforce.

Gordon Murray's low-line Brabham BT55 was designed for minimal frontal area with the tall four-cylinder BMW engine on its side to lower the centre of gravity and the car's cross-section. Its drivers had to lie back with their chins resting on their chests. Though the car was unsuccessful its driving position was echoed on Steve Nichols's brilliant McLaren MP4/4 in 1988.

Below left Reduced frontal area was the aim of the 1986 Brabham BT55, in which Gordon Murray returned the driver to a near supine position.

Below Rory Byrne was the first designer to appreciate that a narrow, pinched nose improved airflow over the front wings and thus enhanced turn-in to corners. By 1988 his B187 trend had been widely copied.

diffusor which once again allowed the airflow to expand. Rigid plastic skirts fitted between the sidepods and the track prevented air from being sucked in from outside, so maintaining the amount of downward pressure or downforce that was generated.

One big advantage of ground effect was that it was 'something for nothing', for the venturis could be designed to exert maximum downforce with minimum drag, whereas the conventional aerofoil or wing would always have a drag penalty when set for maximum downforce.

The second-generation ground effect cars were even more sophisticated, using sliding plastic skirts that could rise and fall whenever a car went over a bump, maximising downforce at all times by maintaining the seal with the ground. However, the result of a skirt sticking up could be dramatic!

Brakes, transmission, suspension

The traditional areas of performance improvement tended to take something of a back seat during the explosion of attention to chassis structure and aerodynamics. Carbon-fibre brake discs continued to be popular and were universal by the end of the decade, while six-speed gearboxes also grew in popularity to cope with narrow turbo power bands, as did transverse units as designers of the new wave of 1988 cars sought optimal weight distribution. The 1989 Ferrari points the way to an intriguing future, however, by using an electro-hydraulic change mechanism in its seven-speed unit, eliminating the need for a conventional clutch and gear lever and enabling the drivers to make very fast up or down changes using small levers on the back of the steering wheel. The sheer change speed apart, the other main advantage is that the driver need not remove a hand from the wheel while changing gear, nor does he have to destabilise the car by declutching during the manoeuvre.

Of the three areas, however, suspension has received the most attention. Inboard mounted coil spring/damper units actuated by rocker arms were the most popular set-up during the seventies ground effect era when clean airflow through the front and rear suspension was such a vital part of the downforce equation, but even before the coming of the flat-bottom regulations all that was beginning to change.

By 1981 Murray had already introduced pull-rod suspension on the Brabhams, while Barnard used a push-rod system on his 1983 MP4/2C. A pull-rod is mounted between the upper outboard end of a wishbone and a rocker arm on the lower end of the inboard coil spring/damper unit, so that when the

Below John Barnard succeeded where others had failed by making a semi-automatic transmission that could win races. The 1989 Ferrari F1/89 used an electro-hydraulic system.

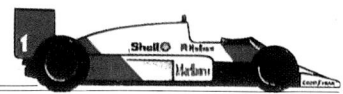

wheel is deflected upwards it pulls the rocker up and activates the spring/damper. A push-rod works the other way round: the rod runs from the lower outboard end of a wishbone to the upper end of the inboard spring/damper, and pushes the rocker when the wheel rises.

The advantages of both systems are that they are lighter because the wishbones can be slimmer (and so marginally more aerodynamic) and need no drag-inducing bulges, once necessary in a nosecone to fair-in the rocker mounting pivots. Rockers could also generate lift.

When FISA banned sliding skirts in early 1981 it stipulated that all cars should have a minimum ground clearance of six centimetres when stationary in the pit lane. The first race under the new regulations passed undramatically, with the FOCA cars still in control despite the teams' fears that the rules favoured the FISA teams. However, Brabham's Gordon Murray evolved a brilliant system for the next race, in Brazil, which turned the rulebook on its head. Reasoning that the six-centimetre rule only referred to the pit lane, he devised a system of hydropneumatically activated dual springs in which aerodynamic pressure eventually over-rode a softer set of air springs, allowing the bodywork to sink the faster the car went. At maximum speed its rigid skirts scraped the track, restoring the lost ground effect. As the car slowed and entered the pits, the softer springs were no longer compressed by aerodynamic load and pushed the bodywork back into its higher position, making the car 'legal' again!

Eventually, less subtle systems were allowed, in which drivers simply pulled a lever to lower their cars the moment they left the pits. The unfortunate corollary of all this was that the cars became markedly more dangerous than they had been with sliding skirts, for now suspension movement had become limited to as little as half an inch to

Left Gordon Murray's 1983 Brabham BT52 made successful use of carbon-fibre brakes for dramatically enhanced retardation, and used pushrod front suspension. The pushrod is visible where it breaks the paint line that runs from the engineer's elbow down to the BT52's nose.

prevent the chassis pitching, and cars jounced and leaped around on the very edge of adhesion and their drivers were acutely uncomfortable into the bargain.

When FISA banned shaped undersides altogether control over wheel movement became essential to maximise what ground effect a car could generate. Travel was thus kept to a minimum and still is, and what suspension there is comes as much from flexure in the locating arms and the tyre sidewalls as from the phenomenally stiff springs that are used. Grand prix cars thus still behave like karts, and the drivers will continue to be uncomfortable.

That desire to maximise ground effect, always strong but stronger still with the post-1983 flat-bottom regulations, inspired many ideas, not least the 'active' suspension system originated by Lotus. Lotus began

experimenting with active ride in 1981, after Colin Chapman's innovative 88 had finally been banned once and for all by FISA. In 1983 Nigel Mansell tested an active-equipped 92, although he was never a fan of the system. When Ayrton Senna first tried it on the 1987 99T, however, he was immediately enthusiastic and it was used all year.

A central computer acted like a brain in conjunction with a system of sensors, the nerves, and hydraulic actuators, the muscles. The aim was to control wheel movement and the ride height with a system that would monitor suspension loadings and body movements and control them to the extent that the car's underside would always remain at the same optimum angle to the road surface, thus maximising its ground effect.

Lotus pioneered active suspension in F1, equipping its 99Ts (below, left) with it throughout 1987. Williams was obliged by Lotus to rename its system, so called it 'reactive'. A key part of the 1988 FW12C package (below, right), it was abandoned after a series of electronic and hydraulic failures; but development work on it continues.

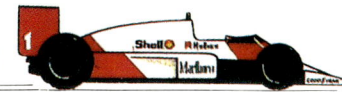
The importance of tyres

Racing tyre development has cost companies such as Goodyear, Michelin and Pirelli millions of pounds during the past decade, yet a set of new tyres is probably the cheapest means a team has to reduce a car's lap times.

When Michelin entered F1 in 1978 they used the same radial tyre technology as in their roadcar tyres, whereas Goodyear were persisting with the ageing cross-ply technology.

Apart from their construction and colour, however, racing tyres bear very little relation to those we use on our own cars. They are much wider and the ones used on dry tracks have no tread pattern because grooves are necessary only to clear water. The tyres have to last only 200 miles at the most, so the rubber is much softer and they thus have a great deal more grip. Usually, it is at its absolute peak for only two or three really fast laps at the most, before the tyres lose their slight edge. Research into methods of tyre construction, different materials and different rubber compounds, to create a tyre that maintains its adhesion and behaviour for as long as possible, is vitally important.

By 1980 the once common mid-race pit stop had become a thing of the past, for few teams were willing to make a voluntary stop which might cost them the race. However, thanks to Gordon Murray, both the tyre change and the fuel stop (the latter banned from 1984) returned in the eighties.

The advantage of a stop is that a driver can

take as much out of his first set of tyres while trying to build up a lead in the early stages, when the car carries its maximum fuel load, before pitting for a fresh set. The replacements do not have to work so hard because the car has used a lot of fuel and is significantly lighter, and they do not have to last the full distance. Pirelli withdrew at the end of 1986, and Goodyear took up a monopoly with control tyres of identical construction for all teams.

When Pirelli returned for 1989, renewing the tyre war, the qualifying tyre also returned. This has a super-soft compound to give maximum grip. However, it lasts for no more than two laps before the grip deteriorates sharply. Its sole function, therefore, is to enable a driver to qualify his car at the highest possible speed. For the race, the car will be set up on much-harder-wearing tyres.

Tyres for everyone. When Michelin and Pirelli pulled out of racing Goodyear supplied the entire field for two seasons, until Pirelli returned to initiate a fresh tyre war in 1989.

The system made the 99T better to drive, since it isolated Senna and team-mate Nakajima from the usual jarring ride of a normal car. At Monaco and Detroit, the bumpiest circuits, Senna won, and he nearly triumphed at Monza too, sliding off under pressure from Nelson Piquet in the closing stages after trying to run non-stop on the same set of tyres. Ironically, Piquet was also driving a car with active suspension, his Williams FW11B using Patrick Head and Frank Dernie's version, which they dubbed reactive ride.

Weight had been the Lotus system's disadvantage, together with the high cost of such a complicated project, and the team did not persist with it for racing in 1988, although they continued research. Williams did persist though, delighted with their success on the FW11B. However, on the less powerful Judd-engined FW12 their lighter system proved unreliable. When it worked it

was effective, but the hydraulics and the electronics frequently malfunctioned, giving drivers Nigel Mansell and Riccardo Patrese high-speed frights. Head is still convinced of its value (and Benetton are too, as they are currently testing their own version) but in the hectic schedule of an F1 season eventually had to abandon it and revert to standard suspension from the British GP onwards. Although the FW12 then finished second in that race, Williams remain enthusiastic about reactive ride and their research continues into what could still prove to be the next major step forward for both racing and road cars.

Although the chassis is the heart of the GP car, its dramatic development during the eighties went hand in hand with similar advances on the engine front during the exciting turbo era. Without either, today's cars certainly would'nt have been able to achieve their current lap speeds.

The Designers

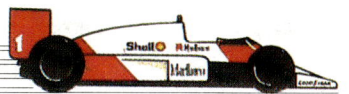

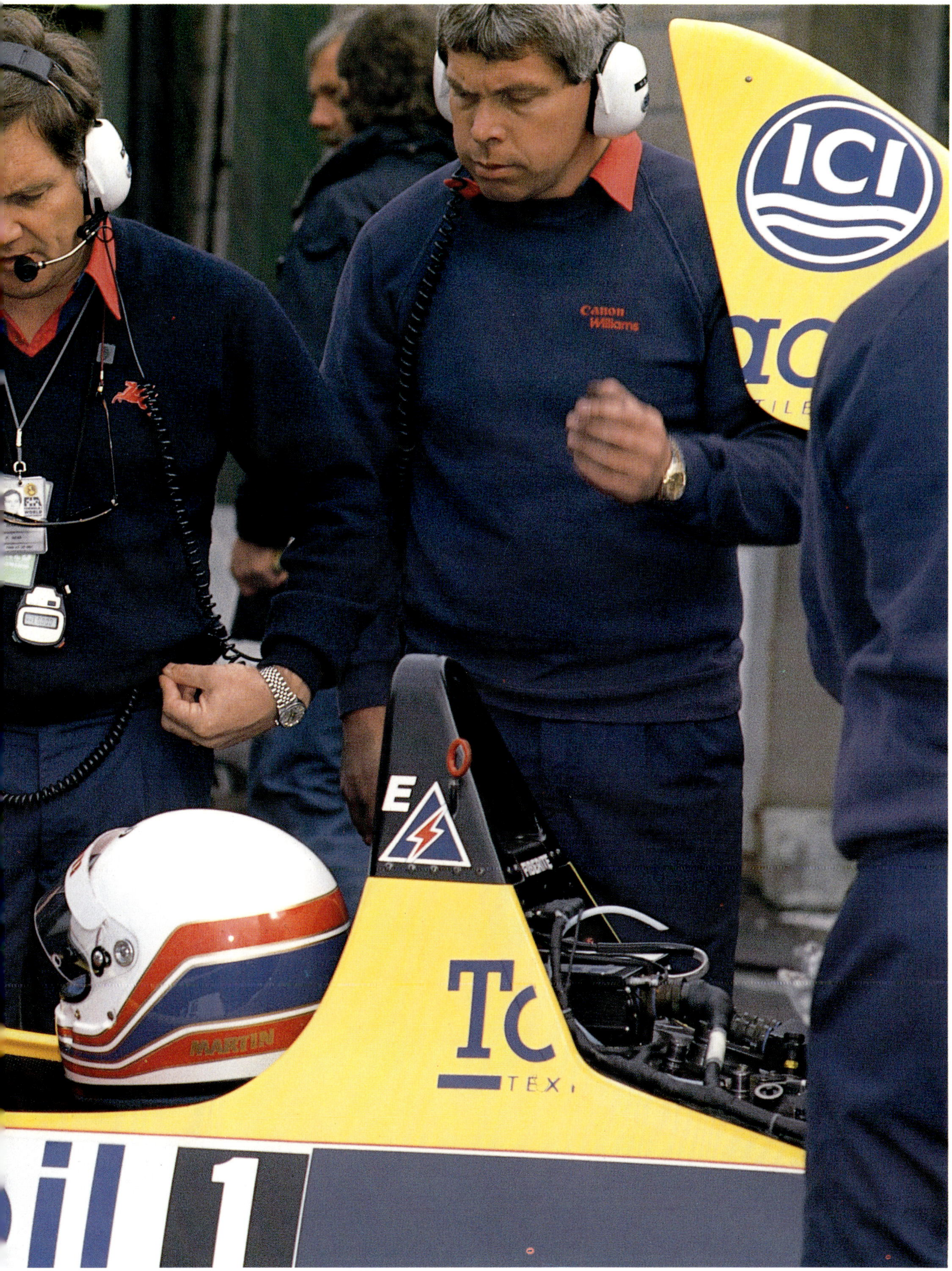
ICI
Canon
Williams
MARTIN
1

The Lotus positions

Preceding two pages
Patrick Head (centre), one of the great designers of the past 20 years, confers with Martin Brundle before the 1988 Belgian GP.

Colin Chapman's record for dramatic developments in the racing world is second to none, even though not all his most famous models were entirely his own work. The founder of Lotus had a true genius for recognising whether an idea was good or bad, and the knack of encouraging his designers to explore theirs. The Lotus 25 was the first successful monocoque in 1962. Five years later he and Maurice Philipe produced the 49, which used the Cosworth DFV for the first time and revolutionised F1 packaging. Their 1970 72 was radical, with wedge shape, inboard brakes and side-mounted radiators. The 78 and 79 models, which he developed in conjunction with Ralph Bellamy and Peter Wright, were further masterpieces that introduced ground effect, while the ill-starred 88, together with the gas turbine-engined 56B of 1971, was further evi-

dence of his lateral thinking. Chapman had been in the forefront of wing development too, on the 49B, and was working on active suspension at the time of his death in 1982.

Shortly afterwards Frenchman Gerard Ducarouge took over as technical director to produce the 94T, 95T, 97T, 98T, 99T and 100T models before leaving at the end of an unhappy 1988. Among his achievements at Hethel were seven pole positions and three wins for the 97T, eight poles and two wins for the 98T, and one pole and two wins for the 99T (including the first for a car with active suspension, at Monaco in 1987). Before that he had designed Matra's world championship-winning sports cars, grand prix winners for the now beleaguered Ligier team, and race leaders for Alfa Romeo.

Left The 1967 Lotus 49, seen here in Graham Hill's hands at Silverstone, was a triumph of lightness and compactness. Both were virtues Lotus had overlooked by the time Gérard Ducarouge (*above*) was called upon to rescue it from the wilderness in the middle of 1983.

THE TEAMS

Cool Head

Patrick Head is every bit as much a part of
Williams Grand Prix Engineering as founder
Frank Williams. He began his career working with Lola Cars before spells with a Super
Vee project and designing the Scott F2 car
which was widely praised in 1972. He
joined in 1975 after further successful free-

60

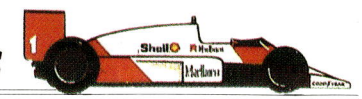

lance spells, stayed working as Harvey Postlethwaite's assistant when Walter Wolf took over, and then left when Frank moved on to set up WGPE a year later. His FW06 was the fastest conventional Cosworth-powered car of 1978, beaten only by the ground effect Lotus 79s, and the following year his second-generation ground effect FW07 is generally accepted to have been the class of the field.

Only poor luck prevented Alan Jones from winning a deserved world title, but the following year he clinched it and just lost out again in 1981. In the subsequent FW08 Keke Rosberg won the 1982 crown.

Head's FW09 was rated as difficult, but it marked the first successful installation of Honda's V6 turbo engine and proved a winner in Dallas. His first carbon-fibre design, the FW10, won four races in 1985 and set Nigel Mansell on the trail to superstardom. In 1986 the Briton was narrowly beaten to the championship by a puncture in the Australian GP in the FW11, but in 1987 Nelson Piquet won the championship in Head's sleek design.

Conservative, occasionally prickly, but an excellent practical engineer, Head is rightly regarded by his peers as one of the very best designers in the game.

Carlos Reutemann in the 1980 Williams FW07. The car took his team-mate Alan Jones to the world title.

The father of carbon-fibre

There is something ironic about the fight John Barnard had initially to get the McLaren MP4/1 – the first full carbon-fibre F1 car – built, for it was such a resounding success that it spawned a new generation of similar chassis and created a revolution not only in F1, but throughout the motor-racing world. Now, customers of lower formula manufacturers can benefit from increased protection for drivers.

Barnard, however, has always been his own man, and he got his way in those early McLaren days, just as he did when he joined

Ferrari and told Enzo Ferrari that he didn't want to work in Italy. Instead Il Commendatore set up an overseas office for him in Guildford.

Like Patrick Head he worked for Lola Cars in his early days, before moving to McLaren to work on the successful world-championship-winning M23 project with chief designer Gordon Coppuck, whom he replaced when he rejoined Dennis for 1981.

From McLaren he moved to the Vel's Parnelli Jones Indycar team in California, his work on the turbocharged Cosworth DFX-

Having left McLaren for a successful spell in American CART racing, John Barnard (inset) returned with Ron Dennis and produced the stunningly successful series of McLaren MP4/1 and MP4/2 championship-winning machines. He pioneered the use of carbon-fibre chassis in F1 while with the British team, and the semi-automatic gearbox after taking over the technical reins at Ferrari.

powered VPJ6B pushing the team to the forefront in 1976. He then moved to Chaparral to work on a new ground effect Indycar for legendary sports car racer Jim Hall. The 2K set new standards.

The MP4/1 was an immediate success, and the MP4/2 series that followed, with their TAG-Porsche turbo engines, swept the floor with their rivals as Niki Lauda won the 1984 championships and Alain Prost the 1985. Prost won again in 1986, but by then Barnard and Dennis had reached the point where there was only room for one perfectionist at McLaren International.

Barnard left, lured to Ferrari where he was swept along in the tide of political infighting as he set about his single-minded goal: to design a new V12-engined car that would win races for Nigel Mansell and Gerhard Berger in 1989—Mansell duly obliging in the pipe-opener at Rio.

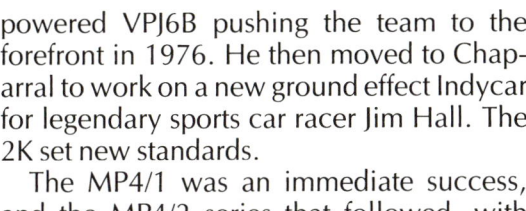

Mr 93 per cent

But for Ayrton Senna's collision with Jean-Louis Schlesser's Williams at Monza, Senna would have won the 1988 Italian GP. Steve Nichols' superb McLaren MP4/4, would thus have won every race of the championship. Still, 15 out of 16 wasn't too bad ….

But for Ayrton Senna colliding with Jean-Louis Schlesser at Monza, Steve Nichols' second F1 design, the McLaren MP4/4, would have won all 16 1988 world championship grands prix. As it was the quiet American's achievement was brilliant as he produced a package of engine, chassis and aerodynamics that was blisteringly fast from the word go and immediately signalled the way the 1988 season was going to shape up.

Through 1986 he built quietly on the experience he had gained working at Mc-Laren in conjunction with John Barnard, and when his chance came to oversee the 1987 MP4/3 project he accepted it eagerly. Then came the MP4/4.

Despite its incredible success, he never became complacent. On one occasion, when it was suggested to him that he was now the cream of the F1 design fraternity, he simply retorted modestly: 'Yeah, but don't forget how quickly cream can curdle….'

Patience is a virtue

The daunting task of designing a totally new F1 car every winter has faced South African designer Rory Byrne five times since 1984. The 1985 Toleman TG185 used Brian Hart's under-rated and under-financed turbo four; the first Benetton, the B186, used BMW's similar engine; the B187 switched to Ford's turbo V6, while the B188 switched again, to the Cosworth DFR; and for 1989 there was to be yet another new Cosworth engine to accommodate.

Not being able to hone a design from one year to the next doesn't seem to worry Byrne, however, and as ever his loyalty lies with the team for which he designed the F2 championship-winning TG280 in 1980.

Unflustered by the difficult birth of Toleman as a grand prix team in 1981, when the bulky TG181 failed to qualify more often than not, he remains supremely enthusiastic about designing racing cars, and although his creations have to date won only the 1986 Mexican GP, he is regarded as one of the most talented men in his field.

Rory Byrne designs are always neat and aerodynamically efficient, and they are renowned for their smooth handling. All they need now is just that tiny extra edge, and Byrne's proven patience is long overdue for its just reward.

Benetton's most successful car to date was this 1986 B186 in which Gerhard Berger won the Mexican GP. Having to produce a new car around a different engine package each year hasn't deterred designer Rory Byrne, whose ideas have set several trends.

A free spirit

Gordon Murray has always been a free spirit, and his unwillingness to run with the herd has always been evident in his grand prix cars, right from the moment his first Brabham, the BT42, was unveiled in 1973. With a curious triangular-section monocoque chassis it looked totally different from everything else and its successor, the similar BT44, was a regular race-winner in 1974.

He made an effective package out of the 1976 BT45 and its bulky flat-12 Alfa Romeo engine and only ill luck prevented it winning races. The BT46 was a much sleeker car despite using the same hefty engine, and the original concept explored surface cooling radiators before overheating prompted a switch to conventional water-cooled cores. No sooner had he assimilated that lesson than Murray came up with one of the most ingenious vehicles ever seen in F1: the Brabham fan car. This raced only once, in the 1978 Swedish GP, and Niki Lauda blew Mario Andretti's ultra-competitive Lotus 79 into the weeds to win. FISA, however,

deemed that the mechanically-driven fan it used (allegedly to cool the engine) actually sucked the air from beneath the skirted chassis, and banned it.

The V12 Alfa-engined BT48 initially tried to eliminate the rear wing with car-length aerodynamic underbody, but that experiment failed too. However, the Cosworth-powered BT49 that derived from it proved highly competitive and took Nelson Piquet to his first championship in 1981, the year that Murray was the first to identify and exploit the ludicrous six centimetre ground-clearance rule.

His BT50, 52, 53 and 54 chassis were all race-winners, the BT52 carrying Piquet to his second title, and he was the architect of mid-race pit stops for fuel and fresh tyres, but his low-line BT55 was a dire flop. This time Murray didn't bounce back. Instead, he moved from Brabham to McLaren International, where his talents are now harnessed creating a pool of design talent that includes Steve Nichols and Neil Oatley.

Gordon Murray's approach produced a series of highly successful Brabhams. This dragster-like BT52, which had all its weight over its rear wheels, won first time out in Rio in 1983, and brought Nelson Piquet his second drivers' title.

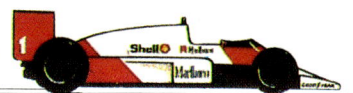
Working in the crucible

Life at Ferrari was never straightforward when Enzo Ferrari was alive, as veteran designer Mauro Forghieri can testify. The quiet Italian worked there from 1961 to 1986, overseeing not only the design of some of the Prancing Horse's most beautiful engines, such as the four-valve V12 of 1968 and the highly successful flat-12 which won championships in 1975, '76, '77 and '79, but also the chassis into which they were installed.

Now, unable to turn his back on the sport, he is responsible for designing the Chrysler-Lamborghini V12 engine used exclusively in the Larrouse Calmels Lola LC89.

When Forghieri finally left Ferrari, following a period in exile on non-racing projects, Englishman Harvey Postlethwaite took over as technical director. After working for March he had first surfaced in F1 with the bubbling Hesketh team in 1973, when he honed their private March 731 into a highly competitive car for James Hunt. In 1975 Hunt won his first GP, the Dutch, in Postlethwaite's Hesketh 308B. After that Harvey moved to Walter Wolf Racing to help Jody Scheckter to second place in the 1977 title chase, and in 1979 he drew the first full aluminium honeycomb monocoque Wolf WR8. He was acquired, along with Wolf's assets, by the Fittipaldi team and was struggling there when the Ferrari offer was made in 1981.

At that time Ferrari was also struggling, having dropped a superb engine into a second-rate chassis, but Postlethwaite changed the company's philosophy and dragged them into the realms of modern constructional techniques. At the same time, he produced the first Ferraris ever to generate any worthwhile ground effects. His 1982 126C2 was an aluminium honeycomb stopgap that nevertheless won the constructors' championship despite Villeneuve's and Pironi's accidents and his carbon-fibre 126C3 repeated that feat in 1983 even though neither Patrick Tambay nor René Arnoux managed to claim the drivers' crown.

Postlethwaite survived the political turmoil of 1985 and '86 which was prompted by poor results. However, after the 1988 upheaval that preceded Enzo Ferrari's death in 1988 he finally packed his bags for home, and at the beginning of 1989 was in charge of design at Tyrrell.

Harvey Postlethwaite produced a winning design for Lord Hesketh as long ago as 1975; but he's better known as the designer who pulled Ferrari out of the dark ages in the early Eighties. His 1982 C2 and all-composite C3 (driven here by Patrick Tambay in Austria in 1983) were both constructors' championship winners.

THE TEAMS

Three to watch

Adrian Newey's *March 881* set new standards for aerodynamic excellence and reduced frontal area.

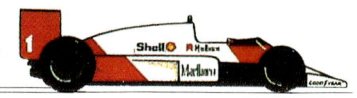

The dramatic profile of Adrian Newey's March 881 drew gasps when it was unveiled and more when it battled past Ayrton Senna and on after Portuguese GP leader Alain Prost months later.

Ivan Capelli didn't win that race, but was an honourable second and actually led the Frenchman for 400 yards of the Japanese GP.

From a team of learners in 1987, March had catapulted towards the front in a tough sport where progress is notoriously hard to make. Newey had drawn heavily on the aerodynamic experience he had gained working with Mario Andretti's Indycar project and from his brief spell with the FORCE Lola F1 team in 1986, and is clearly one of the new generation of F1 designers ready to step into the shoes of Patrick Head and John Barnard.

Following his innovative ATS D6, Austrian Gustav Brunner moved on to co-design the 1985 RAM 03 and was then invited to join Ferrari to design the F187 in collaboration with Harvey Postlethwaite. However, before long he was disillusioned as Postlethwaite did most of the development and then John Barnard came aboard. He left, aggrieved that he had never been allowed to engineer his concept the way he had wanted. He joined the Rial team set up in 1988 by the autocratic wheel manufacturer Guenter Schmid and his ARC 01 performed well enough on a limited budget to finish fourth in the US GP at Detroit, but Brunner and Schmid found it difficult to get on. In 1989 the Austrian faced the future with rival Zakspeed, hoping to find the settled atmosphere he needs to realise his true potential.

Ross Brawn began his career in Williams' aerodynamics department, working under Frank Dernie, before moving in 1985 to the FORCE team to shape their Lola THL-1 and its successor, the THL-2. However, at the end of 1986 he was invited to join Arrows, to design his first full F1 car. The resulting A10 was exactly the sort of practical, no-nonsense car the team needed as they sought to re-establish themselves. Its best results were fourths at Spa and Mexico, but the 1988 A10B version was third at Monza and fourth on four other occasions. With a free rein in designing the 1989 A11, Brawn has the opportunity to put the lessons he has learned into practice.

Left (inset) Gustav Brunner spent time with Ferrari and Rial, for whom he designed the ARC 01. His 1989 ZK891 for Zakspeed has been widely praised.

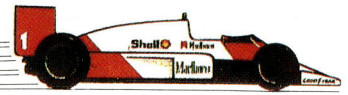

Preceding two pages Old and new. Some 22 years and 155 GP victories separate the old Cosworth DFR, last descendant of the original DFV, from Cosworth's new, type-numberless V8 (right). With a 75-degree vee angle as opposed to the DFR's 90, shorter stroke and larger bore, the new engine was tailor-made for the Nineties. Problems with harmonic vibration in the crankshaft hampered its initial outings, but it produced power competitive with most of its V10 and V12 rivals.

Above, right Ferrari's first forced-induction V6 sited its turbochargers atop the engine. Locations in the chassis sidepods would later become universal.

Below Renault started the turbo ball rolling with a blown version of its 2-litre V6 which made its race debut at Silverstone in 1977.

In no other grand prix formula have power outputs increased as dramatically as they did in F1 between 1980 and 1986. At the beginning of one of its most technically exciting periods, power more than doubled from Renault's impressive 520 bhp in 1980 to BMW's 1300 in qualifying form in 1984-86.

Back in 1951 the 4.5-litre Ferrari finally ousted the 1.5-litre supercharged Alfa Romeo 159 to herald a new era of non-blown engines, and normally-aspirated engines held sway until 1983, when the turbos finally added reliability to their other manifest virtues. In 1988 the unblown 3.5s proved unable to match, let alone beat, the best of the blown 1.5s, but as boost restrictions reduced power outputs to the 650bhp level of 1983 in readiness for the turbo ban in 1989, F1 stood again at the dawn of a new era.

No-one knows how it would have developed if Renault hadn't explored and exploited the little-remembered clause in the regulations allowing 1.5-litre blown engines. That decision—arrived at only after prolonged debate and counter-debate and a great deal of problematic experiment—was to change the course of motor racing history.

If the Renault had worked consistently immediately it appeared in mid-1977, and ground effect had not been harnessed so effectively by other teams, the turbo engine might well have stamped its authority a good deal sooner. As it was, at the start of the decade the Renault V6's 520bhp was at least 50 more than that of the best Cosworth V8s. Yet the aerodynamic lead the British constructors—the *assemblatori* as they were disparagingly called at that time by the *grandee* manufacturers such as Renault and Ferrari—kept them ahead until the power deficit stretched to over 100bhp. After that the writing was on the wall and even in 1982, the last year of full ground-effect racers, any Cosworth team worth its salt was searching desperately for a turbo engine deal.

Though the early turbos were undoubtedly powerful they were exploring new technical ground; they were often unreliable and suffered from spectacular throttle lag and narrow power bands. The potential of the Renault was quickly seen by Ferrari, BMW and Alfa Romeo, however, and Renault's inexperience in F1 was put into perspective when Ferrari's new turbo V6 won two races in its first full season (success for the French manufacturer had taken twice as long). The BMW too, was a winner in its first year, although it had appeared at, but did not compete in, races during 1981.

By 1983 engineers had begun to solve the problems of turbo engine reliability, and from a relatively low 6.7:1, compression ratios began to creep well beyond 7:1, a sure sign of progress. Boost, too, was on the way up as the basic engines improved. Both Renault and Ferrari redesigned their original blocks significantly, to make them lighter and stronger to cope with the increased power. From relatively gentle 2.3/2.4-bar beginnings (one bar being equal to atmospheric pressure at sea level), the turbos were now being blown at nearly 3-bar.

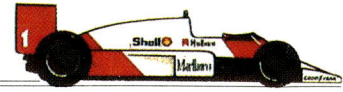

The increase in power was timely, since cars now had to run markedly larger wings to make up for the downforce lost by the new regulations. That really began to hurt the normally-aspirated cars, but the turbos were able to offset the extra drag with their extra power. Lap times were still slower than the frantic 1982 pace, but they would not be for long. The quest for turbo power was about to start in earnest.

The most significant breakthroughs were given further impetus by regulation changes accompanying the flat-bottom rules. FISA could see the way power was escalating and sought means of curbing it. Accordingly, each car was allowed only 250 litres of fuel for each race in 1983, 240 litres in 1984 and a frugal 195 from 1985.

Above Matra's trusty V12 first appeared in 1968, the year after the Cosworth DFV, but had a fresh lease of life with wins in 1981.

The start of something big

In the beginning Francois Castaing never remotely envisaged a grand prix racing role for the two-litre V6 normally-aspirated engine he designed for Renault to use in Formula Two and sports car racing in 1972.

Yet once that unit had been reduced to 1500 cc and fitted with a turbocharger, the French car giant suddenly had the basis for an engine that would start a revolution when it finally raced in F1.

The first turbocharging experiment had, in fact, been intended to improve the engine's power for the Le Mans programme the team had embarked on (which led to eventual success in the 24-hour sports car classic in 1978), but the first F1 version ran as early as the middle of 1975 and was initially intended to race the following season.

A series of teething problems centred on the turbocharging caused considerable delays, however, but a test car ran in the middle of 1976 and, finally, Renault's first grand prix racer since the turn of the century was ready for its debut at Silverstone for the British GP in July 1977.

The grand prix world watched keenly as stories of the project appeared in the media, but the Renault RS01's first outing caused little concern to their rivals as the car qualified 21st and retired early. No doubt many also noted that it would have run short of fuel anyway, even had it been reliable enough to finish.

The turbo route proved a dauntingly difficult one to follow as Renault staggered from one mechanical problem to another during 1978, but there were occasional flashes of promise and a power output around 500 bhp convinced the Regie's engineers they were on the right track if only they could improve reliability and get rid of the terrible throttle lag.

The first breakthrough came when Jean-Pierre Jabouille won the French GP in 1979, and by 1980 there were three other successes to celebrate. The gamble had finally paid off.

Always hampered by their committee management approach to motor sport, Renault as a team stayed in F1 until 1985, and continued supplying engines to customers such as Lotus, Ligier and Tyrrell through 1986. However, beset by industrial problems and disappointed at their lack of consistent success, they then pulled out of racing until announcing their intended return in 1989 with a normally-aspirated V10.

At the time Renault began seriously studying a turbocharged grand prix engine nobody else had given it a second thought, and although other manufacturers subsequently beat Renault at their own turbocharged game, the French company deserve full credit for the ambitious decision which led to wholesale change within a matter of seasons.

Below By 1980 Renault's turbo V6 had been developed into a feared competitor, following Jabouille's maiden win in 1979. Here Arnoux heads for Brazilian GP success.

Electronics to the fore

That lent an added edge to research already taking place into fully electronic engine-management systems. The frequently used technique of cooling an engine by running excessive fuel through its combustion chambers, became impossible in races, but remained a spectacular part of qualifying, where fuel was unlimited.

Now that the regulations effectively called for engines that burned the leanest possible fuel mixtures, to squeeze as much power out of them as possible engineers sought to make them run on the very edge of detonation or pre-ignition, where it was in danger of igniting the mixture in the combustion chamber before the optimum point, to the frequently explosive detriment of its health.

Weber and Magnetti Marelli in Italy, Kugelfischer in France, Bosch in West Germany, Lucas in Britain and Honda in Japan

Turbo fours: BMW's F1 engine (below) employed used cylinder blocks which had few internal stresses, and in its ultimate form produced 1,350bhp on 5.3-bar boost! The design was later taken over by Megatron (bottom) and used exclusively by Arrows until the end of 1988.

conducted expensive development programmes aimed at supplanting the less efficient electro-mechanical systems generally used to that point. BMW in particular had had plentiful problems throughout 1983 as Bosch sought the answers, but steadily they were found and the benefits were immediately obvious.

Electronic control helped eliminate the perennial problem of throttle lag, unless an engine developed a problem. The tiny microprocessors could calculate with complete accuracy how much fuel to inject, and could deliver it in precisely timed milliseconds. Ignition timing was dealt with in similar fashion. Systems were computer controlled, and by changing the chip engineers could alter an engine's characteristics to suit a specific circuit, or to set it up for qualifying or a race.

Normally aspirated engines, of course, benefited just as much from efficient electronic management systems, and all the major manufacturers involved in F1 relished the technical spin-off that would prove so valuable to their production-car programmes.

Hand in hand with the development of sophisticated electronic engine management systems, which helped further to increase compression ratios and hence power outputs, came similarly dramatic advances in fuel technology. Initially most turbos ran satisfactorily on pump fuel of 102 octane, but Winterschall, the BASF subsidiary in West Germany, began research into bespoke fuels. They came up with an exotic brew that used toluenes to make it denser than pump fuel, giving it greater energy and, more importantly, letting the higher compression engine run closer to the detonation limit than it ever could on what FISA considered as petrol. Suitable chemicals were added to toluene to keep the brew within legal boundaries. Water injection, once deemed essential by Ferrari and Renault not only to cool the intake charge but also to promote better atomisation of the air/fuel mix, became a thing of the past. The search for even more power went on.

Power with fuel economy

Allied to other techniques, such as the ability further to tune an engine's characteristics to suit a particular circuit by using small or large turbochargers, the turbo brigade had

developed to the point where it was insuperable. From the breakthrough year of 1983, when a turbocharged car (Brabham) took the champion driver to his crown and another (Ferrari) built on the foundation of 1982 by again clinching the constructors' title, development centred on finding even greater power with increasing reliability and economy. From then on the real battle was for qualifying horsepower on the one hand, and the best race balance of usable power and optimum fuel consumption.

The latter exerted its influence in two ways, mechanical and aerodynamic, and from then on engines were frequently redesigned to suit aerodynamic rather than purely mechanical considerations.

Having developed its 120-degree V6 to the point where it produced over 900bhp in qualifying form on 4.2-bar in 1986, Ferrari brought out a completely revised 90-degree version for 1987. There were several reasons, but the prime aim was to package the engine better within a narrow chassis.

Likewise, by 1983 turbochargers were no longer mounted atop the engine, as in the initial Ferrari V6 or the four-cylinder Hart 415T designed by Englishman Brian Hart, but were neatly housed with their cumbersome intercoolers within the sidepods which had formerly been so vital to generating ground effect.

It was a period of frantic development such as had not been seen in grand prix racing since the début of the Cosworth DFV. One year's successful concept could be outdated within a season, and the research never slowed down as F1 benefited from the massive injections of finance that only manufacturers' budgets could allow.

In search of higher revs, without the broken valve spring penalty that had hampered it early in the eighties, Renault produced the cunning DP (*distribution pneumatique*) valve actuation system on the EF15bis version of its EF4 basis. This opened them via the camshafts in the usual manner, but closed them using compressed nitrogen rather than springs.

FISA's cause for concern over the horsepower race was justified. Ferrari's 120-degree V6, for example, had produced around 580bhp at 11,000rpm in 1981, which was increased over the following four years to over 900bhp at 12,000rpm in qualifying form at 1985's 3.5-bar figure. At the same time the trusty Cosworth DFY could only muster 510 at 11,000, an improvement of around 40bhp over a similar period. By 1986 the V6 Hondas were regularly quali-

Left The secret of many turbo victories was the dashboard-mounted boost button, with which a driver could summon extra horsepower. In frugal 1988 a mixture-richening switch performed a similar function.

fying with over 1100bhp and more than 4-bar boost, while racing with 850 to 900 depending on the effect of a given circuit on fuel economy. The M12/13 upright four-cylinder BMW in Benetton's B186 was probably the most powerful of them all and frequently ran 5.3-bar boost for qualifying. However you calculated it, that gave raw horsepower, generally reckoned to be close to 1300bhp!

This incredible power was still being transmitted through tyres of a maximum width that had been fixed by FISA when 600 bhp was the norm, indicating what terrific strides chassis and aerodynamic development had made in enabling engineers and drivers to cope with such a quantum leap.

Below Renault's distribution pneumatique system of closing the valves was a unique and effective answer to the problem of achieving high revs without breaking valve springs. The EF15 V6 used it in 1986, and it was still employed on the V10 of 1989.

V6 for victory

Proving just how suitable the V6 layout was for a turbocharged engine, TAG-Porsche and Ferrari echoed Honda and Renault in producing race-winning units of similar configuration, while Ford's late-arriving version showed good potential until it was abandoned prematurely.

Of the 141 world championship grands prix run between 1980 and 1988 inclusive, V6s won 99, with the honours split between Honda, 40, TAG-Porsche, 25, Renault, 19 (plus Jabouille's from 1979), and Ferrari, 15.

Curbing turbo boost

The reduction in fuel allowance to 195 litres in 1985 had precious little effect on lap speeds—Keke Rosberg won pole position for the British GP at Silverstone at 160 mph!—so FISA decided on further changes for 1987. Principally, it reduced boost levels to a maximum of 4-bar for qualifying and racing, by means of special pop-off valves. These were to be issued to teams by FISA at each race, to prevent any unauthorised 'development', and were designed, as their name suggested, to pop off whenever an engine attempted to exceed 4-bar.

In practice, few teams had been able to race with more than that anyway in 1986 but the change reduced qualifying speeds. However, computer control and fuel mix progress meant that lap speeds were little affected. After a little initial trouble, and confounding sceptics who felt they could never be made to function properly, the pop-off valves worked satisfactorily all through a season in which the cars proved every bit as spectacular during races as they had the previous year.

As important as the reduction in turbo boost was FISA's decision to ban turbos altogether by 1989 in favour of a 3.5-litre normally-aspirated-engine championship. It encouraged teams to prepare for this by allowing larger capacity non-turbo engines to compete in 1987. Thus the Cosworth V8 was given a new lease of life, this time as the 3.5-litre DFZ which now developed 575 bhp at 11,000rpm. It was, nevertheless, not enough in the light of the 950bhp qualifying and 880 race horsepower that the best turbo teams could muster.

As if sensing this, FISA introduced a brace of Division Two championships, rather unfortunately calling the drivers' the Jim Clark Championship and naming the constructors' after Colin Chapman, neither of whom had ever been second division players.

FISA's new rules, however, were only the first of a two-part package aimed at narrowing the gap between the two different factions, and for 1988, the final year of the turbocharged monsters, their wings were to be clipped further. Boost was further reduced to a gentle 2.5-bar and, perhaps more crucially, fuel allowance for the turbos cut to a meagre 150 litres. At the same time, although turbocars still had to weigh a minimum 540kg, FISA at last recognised pleas for lighter normally-aspirated cars by allowing them to run at 500.

Taken overall, the rules did not succeed in their aim of equalising turbos and non-turbos, but that was more a reflection of Honda's incredible commitment to racing. Throughout their latest F1 involvement the Japanese motor giant made it clear that they would pursue whatever avenues necessary to clinch success. They always used their

Below The pop-off valve, seen here atop Honda's 1988 power unit, proved an ideal means of limiting turbo boost, once initial loopholes had been blocked.

Left As Ferrari toyed with its 1987 engine for 1988, the last year of the turbos, Honda spared no expense modifying its V6, and reaped full reward.

competition programme to train their young engineers in an exciting, demanding and competitive environment. Every aspect of the initial RA163 turbo V6 was thus continuously assessed and reassessed, not just at the end of every season, as might reasonably be supposed, but throughout each season. Several times it was completely redesigned, just as were Renault's and Ferrari's engines, but more than once during a year. The quest for improvement never ceased.

Although Ferrari did make some changes to their 90-degree V6 for the final year of its life, they could not match Honda's wide-ranging modifications to their 80 degree unit. The result, effectively, was a new engine built specifically for the 2.5-bar/150-litre rules, and it won all but one of its 16 races and frequently powered the second place car as well. For that reason more than any other, Honda stayed at the top in 1988 with overwhelming technical supremacy.

With no fuel restrictions, the Cosworth DFR-powered Benettons and the Judd CV-powered Williamses and Marches proved able to run as fast as the other turbocars on most tracks. The Cosworth now produced 600bhp from its lightened and lowered block, even though pre-season experiments with the special five-valve-per-cylinder heads developed in Japan by Yamaha proved curiously inconclusive. The Judd, an enlarged development of the 3-litre V8 Honda had produced for Formula 3000

Above The Ford Cosworth DFR, used exclusively by Benetton in 1988, was the last derivative of the highly successful DFV, but was no match for the better turbos.

Left Likewise, John Judd's Honda-based CV V8 was unable to oust the Honda V6 in 1988 or the V10 in 1989. It was as powerful as the DFR, but much lighter.

racing, was rated at 600bhp too, although at 11,200rpm.

In the past Honda's drivers had had the luxury of a dashboard switch linked to the electronic management system, which allowed them to lean out the fuel mixture as much as possible, to run low or high race boost, or to obtain another 100bhp for 'emergency' overtaking manoeuvres against awkward rivals. In 1988 they could still momentarily enrich the mixture for that 'afterburner' effect, and such niceties often proved critical. Honda did their homework better than the rest, and scored 10 out of 10. A limitless budget, advanced technology and relentless effort clinched yet another championship.

As the turbocharged formula drew to its close, yet another fresh design trend became apparent. The last great explosion of new non-turbo engines had been in 1966

when the 3-litre formula came into effect, and at that time the engine layout dictated the overall shape of the car. BRM's H16 engine was short, wide and heavy, and the chassis designed for it was wide and overweight as its designer attempted to build in sufficient strength. In stark contrast the Cosworth DFV was a light, compact power unit around which Lotus was able to construct the slim, elegant and lightweight 49.

Now weight distribution and aerodynamic profile and cross-section are of such crucial importance, especially at the concept stage of a new design, that cars are tending to dictate the format of engines.

The 1989 formula

Since 1981 grand prix cars have been limited to a maximum of 12 cylinders. Generally speaking the more cylinders, the greater is the piston area and the higher the revs an engine can achieve and, hence, the higher its power output. However, both Honda and Renault opted for shorter vee engines with the unusual number of 10 cylinders, rather than V12s which would then be too long and heavy. Honda in particular examined a number of possible layouts before settling on something totally new to F1.

Ferrari and Chrysler-Lamborghini chose the tried and tested V12 with compact units that make previous versions look oversize, while MGN in France and Life Racing in Italy are conducting research into W12 engines. This layout links three blocks of four cylinders each on a common crankshaft. In essence, the W12 is a wide-angle vee engine with a third bank of cylinders within the vee, and it was used with considerable success in aircraft before the Second World War.

An intriguing feature of the MGN engine, which has yet to race, is its rotary valves rather than the more conventional stemmed valves and springs. Designer Guy Negré noted Renault's success with pneumatic valve actuation and claimed his innovative system allowed the engine to achieve 13,000rpm.

Certainly, high revs are one of the keys to power under the new regulations, and the new Honda V10 and Ferrari V12 have proved themselves to be devastatingly noisier than their turbocharged predecessors. An engine's breathing is also important, which is why Ferrari and Lamborghini have opted for five valves per cylinder. John Judd has produced a special, narrow-angled ver-

Below Honda's RA108E V10 originally appeared with belt-driven camshafts, but had been modified into RA109E specification, with gear-drive for higher revs, by the first race of 1989.

Bottom Like Honda, Renault Sport's Bernard Dudot opted for a V10, regarding it as the best compromise on power and compactness.

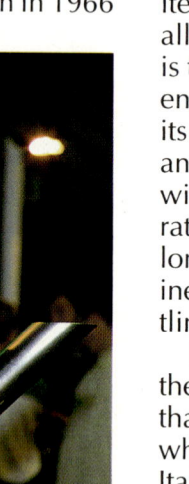

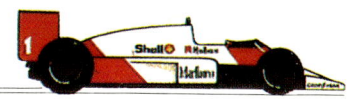

Yamaha 5 Valve

tried and trusted V8 layout, mindful that the DFV V8 beat the 12-cylinder Ferraris and BRMs in the seventies when the experts all championed the multi-cylinder cause. Yamaha, too, have gone for eight cylinders, albeit with their own five-valve cylinder heads.

Fuel is again unlimited under the new formula but engine management systems will become even more sophisticated as designers search for more and more power. It certainly won't come in such large increases as in the turbo era, and every horsepower will have to be fought for. However, Honda's V10 is already giving the same power as its 2.5-bar turbo V6 did.

The turbocharged era of grand prix racing was the most technically stimulating and exciting since the Second World War. A true indication of motor racing's value as a development ground to major manufacturers is their increased interest even though the forced induction that initially attracted them is a thing of the past. Some observers feel that the cost of grand prix racing will now fall with the passing of the turbos, but insiders are all agreed on one thing: the budget levels under the old regulations won't prove a highwater mark, but merely the baseline for the new.

Left Yamaha's five-valve-per-cylinder V8 was ready in time for the 1989 season. Though it proved to be dramatically unreliable in its first outings, few doubted that the Japanese company would get it right eventually, bearing in mind its motorcycle racing pedigree.

sion of his CV V8 just for March, while Lotus, which uses the standard Judd unit, is undertaking a five-valve development programme in conjunction with Tickford.

Ford and Cosworth have again renewed the partnership that produced both the Cosworth DFV family and the 1986 turbocharged V6, and again have opted for the

How turbochargers work

All engines must breathe a mixture of air and fuel, the fuel being atomised with air before it is burned in the combustion chamber and thus forces the pistons up and down their cylinders to produce power.

In a normally-aspirated engine the movement of the pistons sucks in air and the engine is said to breathe naturally. In a forced induction engine the air is forced into the cylinders, so more power is produced.

The two methods of forcing air into an engine are turbocharging and supercharging. Both are relatively simple, but while their obvious advantage is a significant increase in power, both have disadvantages.

A turbocharger is a turbine wheel mounted in the engine's exhaust system. As the engine runs its exhaust gases flow through the turbine and force its vanes to rotate. As they do this they recirculate the exhaust gases, mix them with air drawn into the engine by the movement of the pistons, and force it all into the cylinders. The cycle is continuous and it is almost a 'something for nothing' means of producing greater horsepower. However, many turbo engines

have a delayed response when the driver presses the accelerator pedal, because the turbine does not speed up until the gas flow speeds up. This 'throttle lag' was a major problem with the early grand prix turbo engines, but was eventually cured by sophisticated electronic engine management systems which govern fuel injection and ignition timing.

The supercharger comprises a figure-of-eight shaped rotor which rotates within a casing to draw in air and then compress it. The supercharger had to be driven mechanically, usually from the engine's crankshaft, and fed the compressed air back into the induction manifold to boost power. Supercharged engines were more flexible than turbos because they did not have any throttle lag, but because they were mechanically driven they took power from the engine and so did not produce as much as a turbo.

Interestingly, Ferrari experimented with both turbocharging and supercharging when developing their 1980 V6, opting for the former when the latter proved less powerful and less reliable.

THE DRIVERS

MICHELE ALBORETO

Preceding two pages

Ayrton Senna, top man in 1988 – and for years to come?

Below *Michele Alboreto was given his F1 chance by Ken Tyrrell after a series of promising F2 appearances. He drove his first Grand Prix in 1981 and by the end of 1982 had become good enough to win his first race. He's seen here heading for that victory at Las Vegas.*

When Enzo Ferrari announced his decision to sign up Michele Alboreto for the 1984 grand prix season he likened the curly-haired rising star to the great fifties ace Alberto Ascari. He was the first Italian driver to join the most famous team in motor racing for more than a decade and spent four seasons driving for the Prancing Horse. Yet Alboreto's silky smooth driving style was never rewarded with the success it deserved and, having fallen foul of the complex political forces within Ferrari, he left the team at the end of 1988.

Michele Alboreto served his motor racing apprenticeship in the frenzied surroundings of the Formula Italia national single-seater category from where he quickly moved up into Formula 3. By the time he was 23 he had graduated into the Euroracing F3 squad and triumphed in the 1980 European F3 championship, being noticed by several leading Formula 2 teams as a result.

In 1981 he was signed to drive for Giancarlo Minardi's F2 team, but hardly had he got into the swing of his season than Ken

Tyrrell offered him the number two spot to American driver Eddie Cheever in Tyrrell. Ken's attention had been drawn to Alboreto by an Italian businessman who was keen to sponsor Michele to drive at Imola, Belgium and Monte Carlo. The shrewd English team owner agreed, reserving the option to sign the young Italian on a three-year contract if he considered Alboreto to have the necessary potential.

Michele Alboreto

Born 23 December 1956
1981 FI debut, San Marino GP(Tyrrell), no pole positions, no wins, no championship points
1982 (Tyrrell) no pole positions, I win (Las Vegas), 7th in world championship—25 points
1983 (Tyrrell) no pole positions, I win (Detroit), 12th in world championship—10 points
1984 (Ferrari) I pole position, I win (Belgium), 4th in world championship—30.5 points
1985 (Ferrari) I pole position, 2 wins (Canada, Germany), 2nd in world championship—53 points
1986 (Ferrari) no pole positions, no wins, 8th in world championship—14 points
1987 (Ferrari) no pole positions, no wins, 7th in world championship—17 points
1988 (Ferrari) no pole positions, no wins, 5th in world championship—24 points

Michele qualified 18th for his first grand prix and Tyrrell did not hesitate to take up the option on his services. The Italian quickly earned himself a reputation as a talented and consistent performer, although he had to wait until the 1982 Brazilian Grand Prix before scoring his first championship point with a sixth-place finish, promoted to fourth after Piquet and Rosberg were disqualified.

Although Tyrrell was slow climbing aboard the turbo bandwagon and through to 1985 continued to rely on normally-aspirated engines, Alboreto sustained the team's reputation with two timely victories

at Las Vegas (1982) and Detroit (1983), the last non-turbo F1 victory until turbos were banned at the end of 1988.

Enzo Ferrari was impressed, inviting Michele to join René Arnoux in the Maranello line-up for 1984. Alboreto was delighted: 'It's not just the dream of every Italian racing driver, but of every racing driver, to be offered a place at Ferrari', he enthused. The honeymoon started well: he qualified on pole for his first race with the team at Rio, then won the Belgian Grand Prix in commanding style. But 1984 was the year of the McLaren-TAGs and Alboreto had a dismal season thereafter.

In 1985 things were much better and he won both the Canadian and German Grands Prix, leading the world championship points table for much of the summer before losing the title battle to Alain Prost. In the remaining three years of his Ferrari contract no more victories came his way and, when Gerhard Berger joined the team in 1987, Michele found himself increasingly out of step with the Maranello management. He was particularly outspoken in his criticism of technical director John Barnard and at the start of 1988 stated he would not be staying in 1989 – even if they wanted him.

They didn't. Mid-season, Nigel Mansell was signed to replace him and Alboreto opened negotiations with Frank Williams. Michele thought he had a deal, but Frank changed his mind, leaving the Italian apparently out on a limb. Just before Christmas 1988, he concluded a deal to return to Tyrrell, the team which had given him his break, determined to rebuild his reputation.

Last days at Ferrari. Michele's 1988 season was punctuated by disappointment and tension. Here he stands by his broken-down F187/88C during practice for the British GP at Silverstone.

THE DRIVERS

ELIO DE ANGELIS

Civilised, cultured and good-mannered, Elio de Angelis drove racing cars in the same way that he played classical music on the piano: with a natural fluidity, feel and precision. The son of a wealthy Roman building contractor, he began motor racing as a teenage kartist and, at the age of 19, won the prestigious Monaco Grand Prix supporting F3 classic at the wheel of a Trivellato team Chevron.

In 1979, barely 20 years old, he signed to drive for the Shadow team which by then was in decline. The Italian rising star showed a blend of fire and maturity which belied his youth and, by the end of the year, was being courted by Lotus. He signed up at the start of 1980 to partner Mario Andretti and remained with the team for six seasons.

In 1980 his best result was a storming second place in the Brazilian Grand Prix at Interlagos behind René Arnoux's more powerful Renault turbo. When Andretti moved to Alfa Romeo the following year Elio found himself partnered by Nigel Mansell. A tense rivalry quickly developed between the two men who, though poles apart in personality, were contemporaries each determined to assert his claim for number one status.

Elio de Angelis, barely 20 years old, heads for fifth place in the 1979 United States GP at Watkins Glen at the wheel of the Shadow DN9B. Despite threats of legal action, he switched to Lotus the following season.

In 1982 Elio made his mark in the grand prix history books when he won Lotus's first grand prix since the glorious days of Mario Andretti and the ground effect type 78 four years earlier. After a nail-biting last lap he held off Keke Rosberg's Williams to win the Austrian Grand Prix by a wheel. It was the last Lotus grand prix win ever witnessed by Lotus boss Colin Chapman, who died suddenly from a heart attack the following November, leaving Elio feeling that he had lost a father figure.

Elio de Angelis

Born 20 March 1958; died 15 May 1986
1979 (Shadow) First GP: Argentina, no pole positions, no wins, 15th in world championship—3 points
1980 (Lotus) no pole positions, no wins, 7th in world championship—13 points
1981 (Lotus) no pole positions, no wins, 8th in world championship—14 points
1982 (Lotus) no pole positions, 1 win (Austria), 9th in world championship—23 points
1983 (Lotus) 1 pole position, no wins, 17th in world championship—2 points
1984 (Lotus) 1 pole position, no wins, 3rd in world championship—34 points
1985 (Lotus) 1 pole position, 1 win (San Marino), 5th in world championship—33 points
1986 (Brabham) no pole position, no wins
Killed in testing accident at Circuit Paul Ricard.

In the 1983 season Lotus was in a transitional phase, switching to Renault turbo power with more than a few hiccups, but in 1984 Elio had a simply superb year with the Gerard Ducarouge-designed Lotus 94T. Battling against the might of the Michelin-shod McLaren-TAGs of Alain Prost and Niki Lauda, de Angelis's consistency sustained his title challenge through to late summer before a spate of mechanical failures blighted his progress.

In 1985 Nigel Mansell left the team to join Williams and his place was taken by the gifted Ayrton Senna, a man who clearly had world championship potential. Senna was content with joint number one status for his first season, although he quickly asserted himself as the more convincing performer on circuit. However, Elio won the San Marino Grand Prix, inheriting the victory after Prost's McLaren was disqualified for failing the post-race weight check, and prospects looked quite bright. Senna won both the Portuguese and Belgian races, however, so it was made clear to Elio that if he wanted to stay on in 1986 he would have to accept a subordinate number two role.

It was, effectively, an invitation to leave. Although Senna's star was very much in the ascendant, it was really too much to stomach for the gentle Italian to step aside after six years' hard slog for the famous British team. He left, joining compatriot Riccardo Patrese in Bernie Ecclestone's Brabham-BMW line-up.

The new Gordon Murray-designed low-line Brabham BT55 had a troubled start to the 1986 season, much to de Angelis's disappointment, and the first few races of the year produced little. The week following the Monaco Grand Prix, Elio journeyed to the Paul Ricard circuit, just along the Mediterranean coast, to take part in a routine test session. Going into the 180mph flat-out kink beyond the pits, something went dreadfully and suddenly wrong. The Brabham crashed heavily and grand prix racing's last gentleman player died of his injuries a few hours later in a Marseilles hospital.

After six seasons at Lotus, de Angelis joined Brabham at the start of 1986. He is seen here with the troublesome 'low-line' BT55 being pushed back to the pits during practice for the Spanish GP at Jerez. It was in one of these cars that he was killed while testing at the Circuit Paul Ricard.

THE DRIVERS

RENÉ ARNOUX

At 40 in early 1989 René Arnoux was grand prix racing's current 'senior citizen', yet the zeal which fired this Frenchman's early enthusiasm for the sport showed no signs of cooling, even though the greatest days of his career, achieved with Renault and Ferrari, were now behind him.

Born in Grenoble, the French skiing resort, Arnoux started life as a garage mechanic, but his enthusiasm for motor racing and high-performance cars eventually earned him a position with Conrero, the Turin-based Alfa Romeo tuning specialists. It was not until after the 1972 French Grand Prix that René, hampered by shortage of cash, put all his efforts into forging his own career behind the wheel.

Arnoux visited the rain-soaked Monaco race with a friend who knew Jean-Pierre Beltoise, the man who triumphed that day in the torrential conditions. He sought Beltoise's advice, was steered in the direction

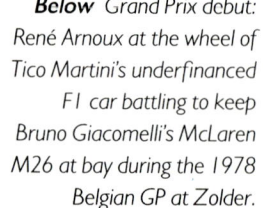

Below Grand Prix debut: René Arnoux at the wheel of Tico Martini's underfinanced F1 car battling to keep Bruno Giacomelli's McLaren M26 at bay during the 1978 Belgian GP at Zolder.

René Arnoux

Born 4 July 1948

1978 First GP: Belgium (Martini), no wins, no pole positions, no championship points

1979 (Renault) 2 pole positions, no wins, 8th in world championship—17 points

1980 (Renault) 3 pole positions, 2 wins (Brazil, South Africa), 6th in world championship—19 points

1981 (Renault) 4 pole positions, no wins, 9th in world championship—11 points

1982 (Renault) 5 pole positions, 2 wins (France, Italy), 6th in world championship—28 points

1983 (Ferrari) 4 pole positions, 3 wins (Canada, Germany, Netherlands), 3rd in world championship—49 points

1984 (Ferrari) no pole positions, no wins, 6th in world championship—27 points

1985 (Ferrari) no pole positions, no wins, no championship points (contested only 1 race).

1986 (Ligier) no pole positions, no wins, 8th in world championship—14 points

1987 (Ligier) no pole positions, no wins, 19th in world championship—1 point

1988 (Ligier) no pole positions, no wins, no championship points

championship to Jean-Pierre Jabouille, but continued in the same category the following year to win the European F2 title at last.

Arnoux's long struggle to Formula 1 was finally rewarded in 1978 when Tico Martini decided to build his own grand prix machine, naturally selecting René to drive it. Unhappily, the little team were swamped by the escalating costs of F1, contesting only a handful of races, but René was rescued by John Surtees for the final two races of the season and offered a contract for 1978.

Wisely, as things turned out, Arnoux decided to wait, banking on being offered the second works Renault turbo alongside Jabouille. The gamble paid off and by 1980 René had become a grand prix winner with victories in both the Brazilian and South African races. When Jabouille was replaced by the gifted Alain Prost in the Renault line-up for 1981, however, René found himself gradually outpaced. In 1982 he won the French Grand Prix, against team orders, then triumphed in the Italian Grand Prix at Monza—the day before it was announced that he would be joining Ferrari the following year!

Initially eclipsed by Tambay, René eventually won the 1983 Canadian, German and Dutch Grands Prix in confident style, the Dutch event at the wheel of the spare car from tenth place on the grid. He retained his place for 1984 alongside Alboreto. Tambay was the one who was dropped, some say unfairly. Thereafter Arnoux's level of achievement became worryingly inconsistent and, after only one race of the 1985 season, he was released from his contract with Ferrari due to a combination of personal problems and a disagreement with Enzo Ferrari.

But F1 hadn't seen the last of this quiet and uncomplicated country boy: in 1986 he returned to the F1 fray with the French Ligier team, for which he has driven ever since.

Leading for Ferrari at the start of the 1983 Canadian GP, Arnoux's 126C3 is pursued by Alain Prost's Renault RE40 and the Brabham BT52s of Nelson Piquet and Riccardo Patrese.

of a French motor racing school, and went along for a trial. René enrolled in the Winfield school at Magny-Cours where his tutor Tico Martini quickly realised that this youngster had above-average talent. As if to back up these predictions, Arnoux won the prestigious Volant Shell competition, setting himself up for a full Formula Renault season the following year (1973) in a Shell-backed Martini.

He battled long and hard throughout a tough 22-race series with Patrick Tambay, the man he was to partner in Ferrari's grand prix team ten years later. Although he won seven races to Tambay's six, he lost the title overall to his rival, and the onset of the 1974 fuel crisis very nearly thwarted any further career progress.

A couple of F2 races at the end of 1974 sustained Arnoux's reputation sufficiently for him to be offered a drive in the newly constituted Renault Europe Championship the following season. He won that series commandingly, finally earning himself a full-time F2 seat alongside Tambay in the works Martini team for 1976. He just lost the

THE DRIVERS

GERHARD BERGER

Below Gerhard Berger's maiden F1 outing was at the wheel of Gunter Schmid's ATS D6 in the 1984 Austrian GP. His second race with the car, at Monza, saw him finish sixth.

There is an outward effervesence about Gerhard Berger which sometimes disguises the sheer steel and determination which suffuses his character. In 1988 he was the only man to put the all-conquering McLaren-Hondas under even the slightest degree of pressure and inherited victory in the Italian Grand Prix when they momentarily faltered. Determined to be the one to profit if McLaren ever hit trouble, he kept up the pursuit at all times and was duly rewarded.

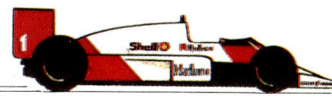

By any standards Berger's ascent to the upper reaches of the F1 community has been meteoric. He first sprang to prominence in the European Alfasud championship, finishing seventh at his first attempt, then breezed quickly through Formula Ford and Formula Ford 2000 before making his mark in the hotly contested 1983 European Formula 3 championship. Although he did not win any of the individual races, he managed a couple of second places to finish joint seventh in the final points table, equal with Martin Brundle.

He then distinguished himself with some energetic drives in the European Touring Car championship at the wheel of a BMW 635. These performances attracted the attention of ATS F1 team boss Gunther Schmid, who duly invited him to Zandvoort for a test session. Berger attacked this task with an over-enthusiasm and confidence which, in retrospect, made even him shudder slightly some four years later. But he certainly made a favourable impression and was invited to drive for the team at the wheel of a second car in two world championship rounds.

On home ground in Austria Berger failed to finish, but at Monza a few weeks later he stormed home sixth in the Italian Grand Prix. Sadly, as he had not originally been entered in the championship as a regular contestant he was not awarded the point normally given to a sixth place finisher.

Barely 25 years old, Berger's racing horizons seemed to be widening dramatically, but his racing career very nearly ended that winter in a serious road accident near his home at Worgl, not far from Innsbruck. He fractured a vertebra in his neck and spent most of the off-season recuperating. He recovered in time to join Thierry Boutsen in the Arrows-BMW line-up, however, highlighting his 1985 season with a fifth place in South Africa and sixth in Australia.

For 1986 he switched to the emergent Benetton-BMW team and really began to mature, displaying considerable flair and expertise. After leading his home grand prix commandingly at the Österreichring, only to be thwarted by battery problems, his great day finally came when he won the Mexican Grand Prix. In searing heat he judged things superbly, profiting by a non-stop run on his Pirelli rubber when his Goodyear-shod rivals were having to stop for fresh tyres two or three times.

By this time Berger's signature was already dry on a Ferrari contract the following year and, after a shaky start to 1987, he

Berger waves his trophy aloft, in company with team-mate Michele Alboreto, after they scored an emotional Ferrari 1–2 in the 1988 Italian GP – the only race of the season that McLaren failed to win.

Gerhard Berger

Born 27 August 1959
1984 First GP: Austria(ATS), no pole positions, no wins, no championship points
1985 (Arrows) no pole positions, no wins, 17th in world championship—3 points
1986 (Benetton) no pole positions, 1 win (Mexico), 7th in world championship—17 points
1987 (Ferrari) 3 pole positions, 2 wins (Japan, Australia), 5th in world championship—36 points
1988 (Ferrari) 1 pole position, 1 win (Italy), 3rd in world championship—41 points

picked up the pace and soon asserted his quality as front-runner, more often than not outpacing team-mate Michele Alboreto. Finally, at Suzuka, he won the Japanese Grand Prix to return the Prancing Horse to the winner's circle for the first time for over two years. A fortnight later he followed that up with a flag-to-flag victory at Adelaide, raising hopes for a serious world championship challenge the following year.

Berger, however, is nothing if not shrewd and, by the end of the 1988 Brazilian Grand Prix he realised the overwhelming quality of the McLaren-Honda opposition. But rather than accept defeat, he rose manfully to the challenge and drove his heart out, scoring second place in Rio and Monaco which were every bit as impressive as the lucky win he was to notch up at Monza. The man has star quality and world championship potential.

ALAN JONES

Alan Jones and the Williams team were thrown together at a time when neither of them seemed to have much to offer. Yet together they rose to become a world-championship-winning force, the Australian driver's blinding determination and tremendous speed interlocking brilliantly with a splendid generation of ground-effect cars produced by Williams designer Patrick Head between 1979 and 1981.

Head, a down-to-earth and practical engineer with little time for the razzmatazz element in motor racing, still recalls the man who won the 1980 world championship with considerable admiration: 'Apart from his overwhelming determination, the great thing about Alan was his ability to lift everybody's morale when things were going badly,' he recalls. 'He acted as an inspiration to the team and that is not a quality displayed by many drivers.'

Alan Jones came up the hard way. He was born into motor racing as the son of hard-driving, hard-drinking Australian post-war hero Stan Jones, knowing both wealth and then deprivation after his father's business hit hard times. In the early 1970s he hauled his way up the F3 ladder with a dogged persistence to finish runner-up to the late Tony Brise in the 1973 British championship, finally making his F1 debut at the wheel of a private Hesketh in the 1975 Spanish GP.

Later that summer he drove for Graham Hill's team, scoring his first championship points with a fifth at the Nürburgring, and then landed a full-time F1 drive for John Sur-

tees the following year. Despite a handful of top six placings at the wheel of the neat Surtees TS19, the outspoken Australian didn't hit it off with his new team boss, and by the start of 1977 it looked as though Alan would be out of work as far as F1 was concerned. Then, somebody else's unexpected tragedy played straight into his hands.

Popular Welsh driver Tom Pryce was killed in the South African Grand Prix and Jones was drafted into the Shadow team as his replacement. A few months later he turned a few heads by winning the Austrian Grand Prix in a car which did not merit being at the sharp end of the field.

People began to watch Jones, just at the time that Frank Williams was regrouping his grand prix challenge for a serious F1 onslaught in 1978. Alan stood out as the obvious man for the job and was duly signed up to drive the neat Williams FW06, Patrick Head's first solo F1 design.

Below Young talent: Alan Jones heads for fifth place in the 1976 Belgian GP at Zolder at the wheel of the Surtees TS19. Some promising performances in this neat little machine helped enhance the rugged Australian's early F1 reputation.

Alan Jones

Born 11 November 1946

1975 First GP:Spain(Hesketh), no pole positions, no wins, 17th in world championship—2 points

1976 (Surtees) no pole positions, no wins, 14th in world championship—7 points

1977 (Shadow) no pole positions, 1 win (Austria), 7th in world championship—22 points

1978 (Williams) no pole positions, no wins, 11th in world championship—11 points

1979 (Williams) 3 pole positions, 4 wins (Germany, Austria, Netherlands, Canada), 3rd in world championship—40 points

1980 (Williams) 3 pole positions, 5 wins (Argentina, France, Britain, Canada, USA), world champion with 46 points

1981 (Williams) no pole positions, 2 wins (Long Beach, Las Vegas), 3rd in world championship—46 points

1983 (Arrows) no pole positions, no wins, no championship points (contested only 1 championship GP)

1985 (Lola) no pole positions, no wins, no championship points (contested only 3 championship GPs)

1986 (Lola) no pole positions, no wins, 12th in world championship—4 points

The partnership immediately clicked, and when Jones got in among the leading Ferraris at Long Beach, Williams realised he'd found himself an extra-special driver. Second place in the United States Grand Prix rounded off their first year together and, with Head's new ground effect FW07 in the pipeline for 1979, the following season turned out to be considerably better. Although Jones's team-mate Clay Regazzoni won William's maiden grand prix victory at Silverstone, he did so only after Jones retired, and Alan more than made amends for this disappointment with subsequent wins at Hockenheim, Österreichring, Zandvoort and Montreal.

This momentum was sustained to win the 1980 world championship, Alan clinching the title with wins in Buenos Aires, Spain (non-title), Paul Ricard, Brands Hatch, Montreal and Watkins Glen. He might well have retained the title the following year, but for a series of trifling technical problems. But Jones continued to drive splendidly, rounding off the year with victory in the first Las Vegas Grand Prix. Then he retired to Australia, despite every effort on Frank Williams's part to make him change his mind.

In truth, he was not ready for F1 retirement. He briefly flirted with Arrows in 1983, then received a tempting financial inducement to re-emerge for a full season with the Haas Lola squad in 1986. But the spark had dimmed and the glory days with Williams were not to be rekindled.

Heading for the title: Jones at the wheel of the superb Patrick Head-designed Williams-Cosworth en route to clinching the 1980 World Championship with victory in the Canadian GP.

THE DRIVERS

JACQUES LAFFITE

Blessed with a delightfully warm and irreverent sense of humour, this Frenchman's interest in motor racing started with him acting as unpaid mechanic for fellow enthusiast Jean-Pierre Jabouille. They later married two sisters, thereby becoming brothers-in-law, not to mention team-mates at Ligier, fleetingly, for the first few races of 1981.

Laffite graduated through Formula 3, bringing his name to the attention of the F1 world with victory in the Monaco F3 classic at the wheel of a Martini in 1973. The following year he got his grand prix chance with Frank Williams, but in those distant days the English team had yet to make their name and were far from reaching the competitive level they were to occupy in the 1980s. On the contrary, it was a financially precarious, hand-to-mouth operation whose cars generally fulfilled a role as also-rans.

For a season and a half Jacques struggled along for Williams, saving Frank's bacon by surviving to finish second in the 1975 German Grand Prix — producing some much-needed income at an absolutely crucial moment — and the two men developed a healthy respect for each other's talents. But Jacques accepted an opportunity to drive for the new Ligier Grand Prix team in 1976 where he remained for seven consecutive seasons.

Using a Matra V12 engine, the Ligier steadily established itself as a reasonably promising contender and Laffite bagged his first GP win in Sweden during the summer of 1977. For 1979 the team switched to Cosworth-Ford power and Jacques used the new ground-effect JS11 to superb effect, opening the season with fine victories in the Argentinian and Brazilian Grands Prix. Thereafter the car's development became somewhat confused and Jacques failed to score another victory until the summer of 1980 when he won the German Grand Prix at Hockenheim.

In 1981 Ligier reverted to using Matra's V12, now under the Talbot banner. It proved another moderately successful season, with Jacques winning splendidly in both Austria and Canada to retain a chance of the world championship until late in the year. After that 1982 proved a sad disappointment and Laffite returned to Williams alongside Keke Rosberg for 1983, the English team now a very different proposition from when he last left it.

Jacques and his family moved to England, where Laffite quickly developed into a great Anglophile, the local golf course catering for his great off-track passion.

At Williams he drove well, despite the fact that he was almost 40 years old. Keke Rosberg, his team-mate, put it in a nutshell when he said 'Jacques is as good as his car. Give him a good chassis and he'll be up with the leaders, but he won't lift an uncompetitive machine further up the grid than it wants to go.' It was a perfect assessment of the Frenchman's talents and Laffite had some very good races, following Keke round Long Beach and Monaco in the neat Cosworth-engined Williams FW08C. Sadly, when the new Honda-engined Williams made its debut the following year, Laffite found himself unable to match Keke's daring and Williams replaced him with Nigel Mansell for 1985.

Laffite returned to his spiritual home at Ligier. The French team were by now armed with Renault turbo engines and Jacques had some excellent runs in both 1985 and the first part of 1986 before a terrible accident just after the start of the British Grand Prix at Brands Hatch. Jacques's Ligier speared headlong into a barrier, breaking both his legs. Although he recovered, and returned to drive saloon cars, Laffite's F1 days were over.

Jaques Laffite

Born 21 November 1943
1974 First GP: Germany (Williams), no pole positions, no wins, no championship points
1975 (Williams) no pole positions, no wins, 12th in world championship—6 points
1976 (Ligier) 1 pole position, no wins, 7th in world championship—20 points
1977 (Ligier) no pole positions, 1 win (Sweden), 10th in world championship—18 points
1978 (Ligier) no pole positions, no wins, 8th in world championship—19 points
1979 (Ligier) 4 pole positions, 2 wins (Argentina, Brazil), 4th in world championship—36 points

1980 (Ligier) 1 pole position, 1 win (Germany), 4th in world championship—34 points
1981 (Ligier) 1 pole position, 2 wins (Austria, Canada), 4th in world championship—44 points
1982 (Ligier) no pole positions, no wins, 17th in world championship—5 points
1983 (Williams) no pole positions, no wins, 11th in world championship—11 points
1984 (Williams) no pole positions, no wins, 14th in world championship—5 points
1985 (Ligier) no pole positions, no wins, 9th in world championship—16 points
1985 (Ligier) no pole positions, no wins, 8th in world championship—14 points

'Happy Jacques' keeps his Ligier JS7-Matra ahead of the McLaren M26s of Patrick Tambay and James Hunt, Emerson Fittipaldi's Copersucar and Clay Regazzoni's Shadow as he heads for a surprise victory in the 1977 Swedish GP.

NIKI LAUDA

Niki Lauda stamped his personality on two decades of grand prix racing in a wide variety of ways, winning three world championship titles over nine years, punctuated by a spell of retirement lasting more than two seasons. He also bounced back after terrible injuries from a fiery crash in the 1976 German Grand Prix to become an international sporting hero whose status transcended the bounds of his chosen sport. But it is as a calculating, objective pragmatist behind the wheel of a Formula 1 car that many in motor racing will recall this great Austrian driver's heyday.

Below Lauda wrestles his BRM P160 around Paul Ricard during the 1973 French GP. Some outstanding performances at the wheel of this good-handling but distinctly underpowered machine earned him an invitation to join Ferrari for 1974.

The odds seemed stacked against Niki Lauda from the start, as far as a motor racing career was concerned. The buck-toothed Austrian kid's parents opposed his first clandestine forays behind the wheel of a Mini Cooper in 1968. But he ran the gauntlet of their disapproval, working his way through the rough and tumble of Formula Vee and Formula 3, finally beginning to be noticed in 1971 when he raised sufficient sponsorship from an Austrian bank to contest the European Formula 2 championship with the fledgling March team.

Encouraged by his own performances, Lauda approached another Austrian bank for backing to secure a seat in the 1972 March grand prix team alongside Ronnie Peterson. But the equipment was not up to

Niki Lauda

Born 22 February 1949
1971 First GP: Austria (March), no pole positions, no wins, no championship points
1972 (March) no pole positions, no wins, no championship points
1973 (BRM) no pole positions, no wins, 17th in world championship—2 points
1974 (Ferrari) 9 pole positions, 2 wins (Spain, Netherlands), 4th in world championship—38 points
1975 (Ferrari) 9 pole positions, 5 wins (Monaco, Belgium, Sweden, France, USA), world champion with 64.5 points
1976 (Ferrari) 3 pole positions, 5 wins (Brazil, South Africa, Belgium, Monaco, Britain), 2nd in championship—68 points
1977 (Ferrari) 2 pole positions, 3 wins (South Africa, Germany, Netherlands), world champion with 72 points
1978 (Brabham) 1 pole position, 2 wins (Sweden, Italy), 4th in world championship—44 points
1979 (Brabham) no pole positions, no wins, 14th in championship—4 points
1982 (McLaren) no pole positions, 2 wins (Long Beach, Britain), 5th in world championship—30 points
1983 (McLaren) no pole positions, no wins, 10th in world championship—12 points
1984 (McLaren) no pole positions, 5 wins (South Africa, France, Britain, Austria, Italy), world champion with 72 points
1985 (McLaren) no pole positions, 1 win (Netherlands), 10th in world championship—14 points

par and the young Austrian almost sank without trace after a disastrous year. None the less, he salvaged his career, displaying considerable salesmanship and acumen to secure a place in the BRM team for 1973. He finished fifth to score his first championship points in Belgium and ran third at Monaco, ahead of Jacky Ickx's Ferrari, until gearbox trouble intervened.

That performance brought him to the attention of Enzo Ferrari, who recruited him at the start of 1974 in an attempt to revitalise the famous Italian team following a disappointing season. Lauda threw himself wholeheartedly into the task of restoring Ferrari to the winner's circle, something he did most ably with wins in the Spanish and Dutch Grands Prix. In fact, only inexperience and a couple of mistakes prevented him from winning the championship.

In 1975, armed with the superb Ferrari 312T, he won five races and clinched the title, 1976 promising a repeat performance until he crashed in flames at the Nürburgring. A few days later he received the last rites, yet within six weeks was back at the wheel of an F1 car, finishing fourth at Monza with his scalp still swathed in bandages. Only his withdrawal from the rain-soaked Japanese Grand Prix spoilt his chance of retaining the title, won eventually by James Hunt after a heart-stopping finale. Lauda was, predictably, savaged by the Italian press for pulling out of that race, but he confounded his critics by bouncing back to win the 1977 championship. Then he left Ferrari, switching to Bernie Ecclestone's Brabham-Alfa squad.

He scored very few victories with Brabham: he won the '78 Swedish GP in the controversial 'fan car' and inherited first place at Monza after Mario Andretti and Gilles Villeneuve were penalised for jumping the start.

By this time his burgeoning airline, Lauda Air, was absorbing more and more of his time, so when he quit the sport abruptly mid-way through practice for the 1979 Canadian Grand Prix, nobody was unduly surprised.

But he still missed F1 and in 1982 returned as a member of the McLaren team. But, unlike Alan Jones, this was no lacklustre return. Niki won his third race that season and in 1984 gained a third championship crown at the wheel of a McLaren-TAG turbo by the wafer-thin margin of half a point over team-mate Alain Prost. At the end of 1985 he retired – this time for good – and now captains his own airline's Boeing jets on a regular run between Vienna and Australia. To this day Niki Lauda remains totally his own man – and one of the sport's most remarkable personalities.

Start of the 1984 British GP at Brands Hatch: Lauda's McLaren-TAG MP4/2 (8) accelerates away alongside Derek Warwick's Renault RE50, aiming for the gap between Nelson Piquet's pole position Brabham-BMW and Alain Prost's McLaren.

THE DRIVERS

NIGEL MANSELL

Nigel Mansell's spectacular determination behind the wheel of a grand prix car propelled him to public prominence in the mid-1980s in much the same way that James Hunt achieved celebrity status a decade earlier. But whereas Hunt won the 1976 world championship, Mansell will be remembered most for his last-minute failure to take the title ten years later. Television viewers all over the world shared the agony of his disappointment as one of the rear tyres on his Williams-Honda disintegrated at 190 mph in the Australian Grand Prix, just as he seemed poised to grasp the world championship.

It was a far cry from his job at Lucas Aerospace in the early 1970s where he had worked on a number of projects, including the RB211 jet engine, before deciding to throw his entire efforts into a motor racing career. Mansell grew up, encouraged by his father, in the rough and tumble of kart racing, a highly competitive environment which has spawned many grand prix drivers. Graduating to car racing proper, he won his first Formula Ford event at Mallory Park in 1976, made his name in the category and then struggled, onwards and upwards, into F3. Along the way he broke his neck and

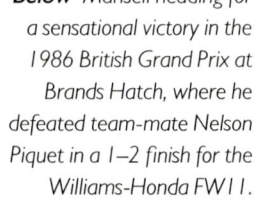

Below Mansell heading for a sensational victory in the 1986 British Grand Prix at Brands Hatch, where he defeated team-mate Nelson Piquet in a 1–2 finish for the Williams-Honda FW11.

Nigel Mansell

Born 8 August 1954

1980 First GP: Austria (Lotus), no pole positions, no wins, no championship points

1981 (Lotus) no pole positions, no wins, 14th in world championship—8 points

1982 (Lotus) no pole positions, no wins, 14th in world championship—7 points

1983 (Lotus) no pole positions, no wins, 12th in world championship—10 points

1984 (Lotus) 1 pole position, no wins, 9th in world championship—13 points

1985 (Williams) 1 pole position, 2 wins (European, South Africa), 6th in world championship—31 points

1986 (Williams) 2 pole positions, 5 wins (Belgium, Canada, France, Britain, Portugal), 2nd in world championship—70 points

1987 (Williams) 8 pole positions, 5 wins (San Marino, France, Britain, Austria, Spain, Mexico), 2nd in world championship—61 points

1988 (Williams) no pole positions, no wins 10th in world championship—12 points

fractured vertebrae in his back, but bounced back with a resilience and determination that marked him out as somebody special.

His dogged exploits were eventually brought to the attention of Lotus boss Colin Chapman, who Mansell impressed considerably during his first test in an F1 car in 1979. Signed up as test and development driver, he was given his chance to handle a third works Lotus in the 1980 Austrian Grand Prix. Typical of Mansell's determination, he drove for much of the race in acute pain from petrol burns caused by the fuel cell leaking into the cockpit, but refused to retire until his engine failed.

In 1981 he became a full-time member of the Lotus F1 line-up, partnering Elio de Angelis, but the team's fortunes were then at a low ebb and grand prix success continually eluded him. Chapman's faith in his talent never wavered, but when the founder of this famous company died suddenly from a heart attack in December 1982, Mansell lost a valuable friend and mentor just when he needed him most.

Nigel stayed with Lotus to the end of 1984, but his driving sometimes displayed a desperate quality, perhaps reflecting the internal tensions with team manager Peter Warr, with whom he found it difficult to get on.

Success did not come his way until 1985, after he had left Team Lotus and joined Williams as second driver alongside Keke Rosberg. Just as his critics were confirming their view that Mansell would never win a Formula 1 race, he scored a well-judged and overwhelmingly popular victory in the Grand Prix of Europe at Brands Hatch. He immediately followed that up with victory in South Africa, finishing the season in sixth place in the championship. Those late-season successes heralded a flood tide of success the following year. His self-confidence bolstered, Mansell sped to five grand prix triumphs in 1986, only losing his chance of the title with that nerve-racking tyre failure in the last race of 1986.

Now acknowledged as a world-class driver, Nigel Mansell delivered more of the same in 1987, a heady blend of breathtaking speed spiced with a handful of errors as well as some mechanical misfortunes. After winning six races in masterly style, an accident during practice for the Japanese Grand Prix wrote the dogged Englishman out of the championship equation with two races to run, handing the title on a plate to his unloved team-mate Nelson Piquet.

With Williams deprived of Honda turbo engines for 1988, the famous English team switched to Judd power and failed to win a single race for the first time in ten seasons. Mansell tried doggedly, scoring a couple of breathtaking second places, but eventually signing a Ferrari contract for 1989 in an attempt to revitalise his championship prospects.

Gritty debut: Mansell at the wheel of the Essex Petroleum-liveried Lotus 81 during the 1980 Austrian GP at Österreichring. Soaked in petrol from a leaking tank, he refused to give up until the engine failed.

97

THE DRIVERS

NELSON PIQUET

Nothing gives Nelson Piquet more pleasure in motor racing than going out onto the starting grid knowing that he has a technical advantage over his rivals. This calculating approach sometimes offends the purists, but the Brazilian knows that world championships are usually won by consistently gathering points, rather than sheer heroism

Above *Nelson Piquet made his Grand Prix debut in the 1978 German GP at Hockenheim, where his neat Ensign failed to finish.*

behind the wheel. He would claim, moreover, that his way works, for he has taken the title in 1981, '83 and '87.

If his father's ambitions had prevailed, however, Nelson might well have scaled the heights of international tennis instead of getting involved in motor racing. Initially he followed in his father's footsteps and became an accomplished teenage tennis player before the lure of cars, karts and motorcycles swayed his ambitions.

Having made a name for himself on the

domestic Brazilian Formula Super Vee scene, Nelson embarked for Europe at the start of 1977 to launch an international Formula 3 programme. Driving a Ralt, he finished third in the European championship before switching his attention to the British scene the following year. He won 13 races during that season, clinching the BP championship and attracting a great deal of interest from several F1 team managers in the process.

He made his grand prix debut for the tiny

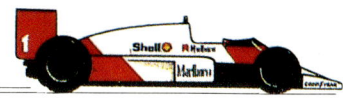

Nelson Piquet

Born 17 August 1952
1978 First GP: Germany (Ensign), no pole positions, no wins, no world championship points
1979 (Brabham) no pole positions, no wins, 15th in world championship—3 points
1980 (Brabham) 2 pole positions, 3 wins (Long Beach, Netherlands, Italy), 2nd in world championship—54 points
1981 (Brabham) 4 pole positions, 3 wins (Argentina, San Marino, Germany), world champion with 50 points
1982 (Brabham) 1 pole position, 1 win (Canada), 11th in world championship—20 points
1983 (Brabham) 1 pole position, 3 wins (Brazil, Italy, European), world champion with 59 points
1984 (Brabham) 9 pole positions, 2 wins (Canada, Detroit), 5th in world championship—29 points
1985 (Brabham) 1 pole position, 1 win (France), 8th in world championship—21 points
1986 (Williams) 2 pole positions, 4 wins (Brazil, Germany, Hungary, Italy), 3rd in world championship—69 points
1987 (Williams) 4 pole positions, 3 wins (Germany, Hungary, Italy), world champion with 73 points
1988 (Lotus) no pole positions, no wins, 6th in world championship—16 points

switched to BMW turbo power, resulting in a mechanically troubled season and only one win for Nelson. But he bounced back in fine style to snatch his second championship in 1983 after a down-to-the-wire battle with the Renault-mounted Alain Prost.

Two relatively bleak seasons followed, after which he stunned the racing world by switching to the Williams-Honda squad for 1986 after Brabham team owner Bernie Ecclestone failed to come up with the financial deal he demanded. Piquet almost won the title again in his first year with Williams, blaming his failure on Williams' not insisting on Nigel Mansell playing a supporting role.

Being edged out by Prost for the championship in the very last race clearly irked Piquet enormously, even though his tactical approach paid dividends as he edged through to take his third title in 1987 with more than a degree of good luck. But he was no happier at Williams and for 1988 signed a Lotus contract, a move which contributed

Piquet's Williams FW11B leads team-mate Mansell, Gerhard Berger's Ferrari, Ayrton Senna's Lotus 99T, Alain Prost's McLaren and the Benettons of Thierry Boutsen and Teo Fabi on the opening lap of the 1987 Italian GP; Nelson went on to win.

Ensign team at Hockenheim, where he retired, before moving on to handle a private McLaren in the Austrian, Dutch and Italian races. Finally, in the Canadian Grand Prix, he rounded off the year with a drive for Brabham, laying the groundwork for a partnership which lasted for seven seasons.

Following Niki Lauda's abrupt—and, as it turned out, temporary—retirement late in 1979, Piquet found himself elevated to the status of Brabham team leader. The following year he won his first grand prix at Long Beach (California) in a new Ford-engined Brabham BT49 and went on to score further triumphs in the Dutch and Italian races. Despite his novice status, he finished runner-up in the championship behind Alan Jones.

The following year Piquet won his first world title, edging out Carlos Reutemann by a single point in a tense, sweltering finale at Las Vegas. Then for 1982 Brabham

to Frank's team losing its Honda engine supply contract.

However, he found no joy at Lotus and had a disastrous season, unable to sustain much motivation behind the wheel of a demonstrably uncompetitive car. Reasoning that not even a super-human effort would get him on terms with the dominant McLarens, he took things steadily for much of the time. Only time will tell whether Nelson Piquet can regain some semblance of his former status.

DIDIER PIRONI

Driven on by the burning ambition to become his country's first world champion, this dour and pragmatic Frenchman brought a clinical and objective approach to his motor racing. In that respect he was very like Ayrton Senna, but Pironi always had his ice-cool temperament under firm rein. After Gilles Villeneuve was killed early in 1982 he assumed the Ferrari team leadership to brilliant effect, but his world championship challenge ended abruptly in a massive accident during practice at Hockenheim. His mount cartwheeled over the back of Alain Prost's Renault, leaving Pironi with serious leg injuries that ended his racing career.

Inspired by the racing exploits of his cousin, the late José Dolhem, Didier's engineering studies took second place to a deep-seated enthusiasm for motor racing. In 1972 he won first prize in the Volant Elf competition on the same day as his compatriot René Arnoux won the similar Volant Shell contest at Magny-Cours. In 1973 he contested the national Formula Renault championship, finishing sixth, but returned to win the title with his own team the following year.

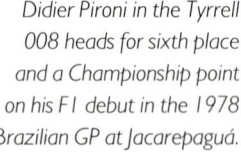

Didier Pironi in the Tyrrell 008 heads for sixth place and a Championship point on his F1 debut in the 1978 Brazilian GP at Jacarepaguá.

France had a really strong motor racing infrastructure at the time, but Pironi's graduation to the more senior Formula Renault Europe contest was fraught with disappointment in 1975. He stayed in this category in '76, winning 12 of the 16 races, then moved into F2 with Martini. He finished third in the European championship behind Arnoux and Eddie Cheever but, more significantly, had a guest drive for Martini in the F3 classic supporting the Monaco Grand Prix. He won handsomely, in the process attracting the attention of Ken Tyrrell, who signed him to

Didier Pironi

Born 26 March 1952; died 23 August 1987

1978 First GP: Brazil (Tyrrell), no pole positions, no wins, 15th in world championship—7 points

1979 (Tyrrell) no pole positions, no wins, 10th in world championship—14 points

1980 (Ligier) 2 pole positions, 1 win (Belgium), 5th in world championship—32 points

1981 (Ferrari) no pole positions, no wins, 13th in world championship—9 points

1982 (Ferrari) 2 pole positions, 2 wins (San Marino, Netherlands), 2nd in world championship—39 points

partner Patrick Depailler in his F1 team the following year.

He did well during that first F1 season, scoring points in four of his first six races. The second half of the season was less successful for Didier, but he at least had the consolation of winning the Le Mans 24-hour classic, sharing the victorious Renault with Jean-Pierre Jaussaud. Renault wanted him to join their F1 team for '79, but Tyrrell wouldn't release him from his contract, so he spent another year with Ken before moving to Ligier.

At Ligier he won his first grand prix in Belgium, beating Alan Jones's Williams comfortably. He led Jones again at Monaco, where both retired, and finished second to the Australian at Paul Ricard.

At the end of the year the retiring Jody Scheckter recommended Pironi to succeed him at Ferrari and Didier duly joined the Italian team as Villeneuve's partner. He seldom looked in Gilles's class, however, and a fourth place at Monaco was the best he could manage in a year when Villeneuve notched up two grand prix wins.

The 1982 season began on a promising note, with Ferrari dominating the San Marino Grand Prix at Imola after the predominantly British-based teams, aligned with the influential Formula One Constructors' Association, boycotted the race in a complex rule dispute with the sport's governing body. Pironi won, slipstreaming past Villeneuve on the last lap, but against team orders in Gilles's view. The Canadian driver, who'd previously regarded Pironi as a friend, never spoke to him again. A fortnight later Villeneuve was killed in practice for the Belgian Grand Prix.

Pironi went on to win the Dutch Grand Prix in masterly style before that tragic Hockenheim accident cut short his season. Ahead lay dozens of painful operations over the years to repair his shattered legs and predictions about his planned return to the cockpit seemed increasingly over-optimistic.

Restless for a sporting challenge, Pironi turned his hand to the equally spectacular and often dangerous sport of powerboat racing, only to die, along with two colleagues, in an accident off the Isle of Wight in the summer of 1987.

Pironi's Ferrari 126C2 (left) outbrakes Alain Prost's Renault to take the lead of the 1982 Dutch GP at Zandvoort. It was to be the final victory of Didier's F1 career.

THE DRIVERS

ALAIN PROST

In years to come the grand prix history books will assess Alain Prost as the pivotal personality of the 1980s. By the end of 1988 the pleasantly unassuming Frenchman with the impish sense of humour had won only two world championship titles, but with 35 grand prix victories to his credit had comfortably eclipsed Jackie Stewart's previous record and seemed set to score an eventual total which might well never be matched.

Above Prost at the wheel of the McLaren M29 in the 1980 Brazilian GP at Interlagos, where he took fifth place in only his second GP outing. He had already scored a sixth place finish on his debut at Buenos Aires.

Beyond question, Prost displayed the Midas touch from the very start of his career. He won the 1973 karting world championship, three years later displayed a similar mastery of the European Formula Renault series and in 1979 clinched the European F3 championship. The way was clearly open for grand prix stardom and, after McLaren offered him a test drive at the end of 1979, director Teddy Mayer signed him on the spot.

Although 1980 was one of the most disappointing seasons overall in McLaren history, Alain scored championship points on his first two outings for the team. However, it was a frustrating year for the young Frenchman and, when offered a Renault seat for 1981, he quickly took it, despite a certain amount of legal wrangling with McLaren. Almost immediately he began to reel off the victories, yet the drivers' title consistently eluded him. The cars were often unreliable and, after a major disagreement, he left the French team at the end of 1983.

It was a timely decision. Over at McLaren

Alain Prost

Born 24 February 1955
1980 First GP: Argentina (McLaren), no pole positions, no wins, 15th in world championship—5 points
1981 (Renault) 2 pole positions, 3 wins (France, Netherlands, Italy), 5th in world championship—43 points
1982 (Renault) 5 pole positions, 2 wins (South Africa, Brazil), 4th in world championship—34 points
1983 (Renault) 3 pole positions, 4 wins (France, Belgium, Britain, Austria), 2nd in world championship—57 points
1984 (McLaren) 3 pole positions, 7 wins (Brazil, San Marino, Monaco, Germany, Netherlands, Europe, Portugal), 2nd in world championship—71 points
1985 (McLaren) 2 pole positions, 5 wins (Brazil, Monaco, Britain, Austria, Italy), world champion with 73 points
1986 (McLaren) 1 pole position, 4 wins (San Marino, Monaco, Austria, Australia), world champion with 72 points
1987 (McLaren) no pole positions, 3 wins (Brazil, Belgium, Portugal), 4th in world championship—46 points
1988 (McLaren) 1 pole position, 7 wins (Brazil, Monaco, Mexico, France, Portugal, Spain, Australia), 2nd in world championship with 84 points

John Watson had not yet finalised his contract for the following year and the team's management quickly offered Prost the chance of running alongside Niki Lauda. The Frenchman signed up without hesitation. It proved absolutely the correct choice. With its new Porsche-built TAG turbo engine ready to race, the 1984 McLaren proved to be in a class of its own; but although Alain won seven races to Niki's five, Lauda took the title by the scant margin of half a point.

In 1985 Prost left nothing to chance, winning five grands prix to clinch that long-awaited title. He did it again the following year, the first driver since Jack Brabham in 1959 and 60 to take consecutive titles. Prost's amazingly smooth driving technique and mechanical empathy marked him out as the natural successor to Niki Lauda as the best all-round F1 'technocrat'.

In 1987 lack of development on the TAG/Porsche engine left Prost handicapped, but he drove brilliantly throughout the year to win three more races. In the last of them, at Estoril in Portugal, he relentlessly hounded Gerhard Berger into a spin only three laps from the chequered flag, surging through to beat Jackie Stewart's 13-year record of 27 wins. In the 1988 season Prost faced the biggest challenge of his career when the gifted Brazilian Ayrton Senna was signed to drive alongside him and McLaren switched to Honda power in the last year before turbo-charged engines were finally outlawed. The combination of these two gifted drivers and the new McLaren-Honda was such an advantage over the opposition that between them they won 15 out of 16 races, turning the world championship into their own personal playground.

It speaks volumes for Prost that after almost a decade in F1 he could still improve his standard to combat the ascetic Senna, whose level of commitment and determination seemed almost chilling sometimes. He took fewer calculated gambles in heavy traffic than his youthful rival, and found it impossible to conceal his dislike of racing in the rain. But although the title eventually went to the younger man, Prost continued to drive just as expertly and promises to be just as much a championship contender in 1989.

Glorious moment: Alain clinches his second World Championship with victory in the 1986 Australian GP. It was the first time a driver had scored a back-to-back title success since Jack Brabham's two Championships for Cooper in 1959 and 1960.

CARLOS REUTEMANN

This Argentinian driver remained something of an enigma throughout his long and distinguished Formula 1 career, combing flashes of dazzling genius behind the wheel with disappointingly lacklustre showings. Off-track he had a gentle, thoughtful and charming personality which was often concealed behind a mask of deep thought and concentration.

He first came to Europe in 1970 to contest Formula 2 for a team sponsored by the Automobile Club of Argentina. He only just missed the 1971 European F2 title, losing out to Ronnie Peterson in the final race of the season, but quickly moved up into F1 with Bernie Ecclestone's Brabham team the following season.

It was not until 1974 that Brabham designer Gordon Murray produced a machine that could do justice to Reutemann's talent, however: the elegant BT44, in which he notched up commanding victories in the South African, Austrian and United States grands prix. The following year he won the German Grand Prix at the Nürburgring in a development of this Cosworth-engined Brabham, but when Ecclestone negotiated a deal to use the Alfa Romeo flat-12 engine for 1976, Reutemann lost heart. Disappointed with the performance of the new cars, he negotiated a release from his Brabham contract and signed for Ferrari.

Carlos Reutemann and Brabham boss Bernie Ecclestone confer before the start of the 1974 United States GP. The dusky Argentinian won this race commandingly at the wheel of his BT44.

He only raced once, at Monza, for the Italian team that year, but lined up alongside Niki Lauda for a full season in 1977. Lauda and Reutemann didn't really hit it off together, possibly because of their diametrically different personalities. Reutemann won only the Brazilian Grand Prix that year, but once Lauda had triumphed brilliantly at Rio, Long Beach, Brands Hatch and Watkins Glen the following year. In 1979 he moved to Lotus, with disappointing results, after which he went to Williams as team-mate to Alan Jones.

Again Reutemann found himself paired alongside a man with whom he had little in common. Jones was extrovert, sometimes abrasive whereas Carlos was an introvert, perhaps over-sensitive. He was certainly too

Carlos Reutemann

Born 12 April 1942

1972 First GP: Argentina (Brabham), 1 pole position, no wins, 16th in world championship—3 points

1973 (Brabham) no pole positions, no wins, 7th in world championship—16 points

1974 (Brabham) 1 pole position, 3 wins (South Africa, Austria, USA), 6th in world championship—32 points

1975 (Brabham) no pole positions, 1 win (Germany), 3rd in world championship—37 points

1976 (Brabham/Ferrari) no pole positions, no wins, 16th in world championship—3 points

1977 (Ferrari) no pole positions, 1 win (Brazil), 4th in world championship—42 points

1978 (Ferrari) 2 pole positions, 4 wins (Brazil, Long Beach, Britain, US East), 3rd in world championship—48 points

1979 (Lotus) no pole positions, no wins, 6th in world championship—20 points

1980 (Williams) no pole positions, 1 win (Monaco), 3rd in world championship—42 points

1981 (Williams) 2 pole positions, 2 wins (Brazil, Belgium), 2nd in world championship—49 points

1982 (Williams) no pole positions, no wins, 15th in world championship—6 points. Retired after two races

good to be content with the nominal number two status at Williams. In 1980 he won a single grand prix, at Monaco, after Jones and Didier Pironi's Ligier retired in front of him, but in 1981 he mounted the strongest championship challenge of his career. He opened the year by winning the Brazilian Grand Prix against team orders, ignoring pit signals to drop back behind Jones. He was penalised financially, but Carlos couldn't have cared less. In his view, he was a racer, and racers don't throw away victories.

After a succession of good performances, including another victory in Belgium, he arrived at Las Vegas for the final race of the season on the threshold of the championship. A blindingly quick lap qualified him commandingly on pole position, but when the starting light blinked green Reutemann unaccountably simply capitulated. Fading to eighth place, he walked away muttering that the car had not been handling properly,

but, in truth, it was an inexplicable performance. The only explanation seemed to be that, in some perverse way, he didn't really want to win the championship at all.

Two races into the 1982 season Carlos Reutemann retired from the cockpit for good. He never went back on that spontaneous decision even though he subsequently admitted he gave up too soon. Quite why he did so is a secret that will probably never be revealed.

Carlos's sole Monaco victory came in the Williams FW07B in 1980 – but only after team-mate Alan Jones and Didier Pironi (Ligier) retired from the race.

KEKE ROSBERG

It is a matter of some pride to Keke Rosberg that he earned money from his motor racing almost from the start. The moustachioed Finn's reputation was forged during the early 1970s in the hectic surroundings of Formula Vee, consolidated in F2 and F/Atlantic before he earned his promotion to F1 at the start of 1978 when he drove the bulky Theodore in the South African Grand Prix.

Keke really made his name with victory in the non-championship 1978 Silverstone International Trophy race, however, keeping control in monsoon conditions that forced many of his more exalted rivals to pirouette into ignominious retirement. When James Hunt retired mid-season the following year Rosberg took his place in the Wolf Racing team, staying on when it amalgamated with former champion Emerson Fittipaldi's organisation at the start of 1980.

Unfortunately Rosberg's two-year stint with Fittipaldi Automotive proved a major setback to his career prospects. Shortage of sponsorship was a major problem and the machinery began to suffer. The team failed to score a single world championship point in 1981 and Keke qualified for only one of his last seven races. Yet Rosberg's self-belief never wavered and, after Alan Jones abruptly retired, a test session at Paul Ricard was all the Williams team needed to be convinced that the Finn was the driver for them.

Keke signed up as number two to Carlos Reutemann, only to find himself propelled into the team leadership after a couple of races when the Argentinian also retired. Now armed with a competitive car, Rosberg could go motor racing with a vengeance, although his flamboyant, opposite-lock

Rosberg sits patiently in the cockpit of the Ron Tauranac-designed Theodore during practice for the 1978 Silverstone International Trophy. The weather was very different on race day, Keke surfing to victory in torrential rain ahead of Emerson Fittipaldi's Copersucar.

Keke Rosberg

Born 6 December 1948
1978 First GP: South Africa (Theodore), no pole positions, no wins, no championship points
1979 (Wolf) no pole positions, no wins, no championship points
1980 (Fittipaldi) no pole positions, no wins, 10th in world championship—6 points
1981 (Fittipaldi) no pole positions, no wins, no championship points
1982 (Williams) 1 pole position, 1 win (Swiss), world champion with 44 points
1983 (Williams) 1 pole position, 1 win (Monaco), 5th in world championship—27 points
1984 (Williams) no pole positions, 1 win (Dallas), 8th in world championship—20.5 points
1985 (Williams) 2 pole positions, 2 wins (Detroit, Australia), 3rd in world championship—40 points
1986 (McLaren) 1 pole position, no wins, 6th in world championship—22 points

driving style was sometimes at odds with designer Patrick Head's concept of how a grand prix car should be handled. His first championship win was in the Swiss Grand Prix at Dijon-Prenois and he sustained this momentum to snatch the world title in the final race of the season at Las Vegas.

The Williams team were late on the turbo bandwagon and had no such powerful engine in 1983, but Rosberg still rewarded them with a brilliant victory in the Monaco Grand Prix. Gambling correctly that the rain-slicked track surface would dry out quickly, he started on slick tyres and out-ran the more powerful opposition in an awesome display of lightning reflexes. He failed to win another race that season, but by dint of some heroic motoring kept the naturally-aspirated Williams within sight of the turbos on all but the very fastest circuits.

Armed with Honda turbo power in '84, Keke fought an uphill battle against the all-conquering McLaren-TAGs, but gave the Williams team its first turbocharged win in the searing Texas heat in the one-off Dallas Grand Prix. While most of his top drawer opposition were either sliding into walls or retiring with heat exhaustion, Rosberg kept his cool to win probably the most impressive victory of his career.

At the start of '85 Keke was lukewarm about Nigel Mansell joining Williams as his team-mate and with typical candour, said so. Later, with characteristic honesty, Rosberg conceded he had been wrong. He won at Detroit and Adelaide in the Williams-Honda, but early on decided to switch to McLaren in 1986 for a final stab at another title.

'I thought I was the fastest driver in the world, until I went to McLaren with Alain Prost,' he later remarked wryly. That final season proved a disappointment, with no wins coming his way, but Keke did not go back on his decision to retire. Happily, he remains active on the grand prix scene, a cheerful chain smoker who loves keeping abreast of the latest gossip.

Waiting for the off at Detroit in 1985, where Keke scored a fine victory at the wheel of the Williams-Honda FW10. He would later win again at Adelaide, before switching to McLaren for 1986.

THE DRIVERS

AYRTON SENNA

Probably the most intensely committed grand prix driver of his generation, Ayrton Senna realised his ambition in 1988 by winning a record eight grand prix in a single season to clinch his first world championship. To those who had known him from early in his career it was the logical outcome of a perfectionist approach to his chosen sport by a remarkably gifted performer.

The son of a wealthy Sao Paulo businessman who built him a kart when he was

Senna's Toleman TG183B – minus nose cover – leads team-mate Johnny Cecotto in the 1983 South African GP. Ayrton finished sixth in this, his second F1 outing.

only four years old, Ayrton had been racing such devices very seriously for eight years by the time he exploded onto the national British Formula Ford scene in 1981. Instantly this quiet and shy young Brazilian proved that he had enormous talent. At the wheel of a Van Diemen he took two of the British championships by storm, winning 12 times in 20 outings. Briefly demoralised by shortage of sponsorship, he moved up into Formula Ford 2000 the following year with similarly spectacular results.

In 1983 he won the British F3 title after a season-long battle with Martin Brundle, then catapulted into grand prix racing with Toleman. He scored a championship point in his second race and it soon became clear

that Senna was a potential winner, even at this early stage of his career. This was underlined dramatically when he forced his Toleman through to a second place at Monaco and was right on Alain Prost's tail when the race was brought to a premature halt in torrential rain. Thereafter it was clear that his talent exceeded the Toleman's potential and, by the time he rounded off the season with a splendid third behind the McLarens of Prost and Lauda at Estoril, he had already decided on a move to Lotus for 1985.

It was the correct decision. Senna's first grand prix win was on his next return to Estoril, in monsoon conditions that made even Alain Prost spin into retirement on the straight. He followed this with a succession

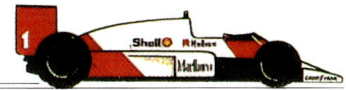

of superb performances in the Renault-engined 97T, including another victory at Spa in the Belgian Grand Prix. In 1986 he started from pole position in no fewer than nine races, beating Nigel Mansell's Willaims-Honda by one-hundredth of a second to win the Spanish Grand Prix, and then adding Detroit to his tally of triumphs, despite being delayed with a puncture.

Despite these successes it was becoming

Ayrton Senna

Born 21 March 1960
1984 First GP: Brazil (Toleman), no pole positions, no wins, 9th in world championship—13 points
1985 (Lotus) 7 pole positions, 2 wins (Portugal, Belgium), 4th in world championship—38 points
1986 (Lotus) 9 pole positions, 2 wins (Spain, Detroit), 4th in world championship—55 points
1987 (Lotus) 1 pole position, 2 wins (Monaco, Detroit), 3rd in world championship—57 points
1988 (McLaren) 13 pole positions, 8 wins (San Marino, Canada, Detroit, Britain, Germany, Hungary, Belgium, Japan), world champion with 87 points

apparent to Senna that as long as Williams had Honda power, the only to beat them was to join them. So Lotus contracted with the Japanese company for 1987 and Ayrton started the year feeling optimistic. Sadly, though, the Lotus 99T simply wasn't in the same aerodynamic league as the Williams, as Senna was quick to appreciate. He slogged away with characteristic single mindedness, but could only score two wins, at Monaco and Detroit. The answer, quite clearly, was to accept an offer from McLaren, who were to replace Williams as one of the Honda-supplied teams in 1988.

Partnering Alain Prost was obviously going to be an enormous challenge for Senna, yet the Brazilian raided what had become the Frenchman's own personal domain and came away with first prize. He won the San Marino, Canadian, Detroit, British, German, Hungarian, Belgian and Japanese Grands Prix—and would have added Monaco and Italy if minor driving errors had not eliminated him from both. He also stalled on the grid in Japan, but managed to bump-start the engine, which he drove with a unique verve, climbing back from 14th place to win, clinching the title.

In early 1989 he is maturing with every race. If he can control the slightly impetuous streak in his driving, this ascetic Brazilian could well enjoy enormous success.

Mastery: leading the opening lap of the 1988 Hungarian GP with Nigel Mansell and Riccardo Patrese chasing hard in their Williams FW12-Judds. He won by a couple of lengths from team-mate Prost.

109

GILLES VILLENEUVE

Above Meteoric debut: Gilles Villeneuve in the McLaren M23 with which he rocked the establishment on his first F1 outing in the 1977 British GP. But for a faulty cockpit gauge, he would almost certainly have finished fourth.

This genial, easy-going French-Canadian was one of those rare personalities who became a legend in their own lifetime. Cast in the heroic mould, fearless and undaunted, his approach was the subject for more debate than that of any of his contemporaries. There were those who thought he was wonderful, embodying all the uninhibited traditional values which makes motor racing so spectacular. Others, less romantic, loftily dismissed his opposite-lock, tyre-smoking antics as an unnecessary waste of energy.

Whatever one's verdict, he was undoubtedly a great driver who knew no other way to drive than flat-out. Personal risk didn't seem to be part of the equation. From the time that he first began racing snowmobiles in his native Quebec at the age of eight, Gilles displayed an uninhibited natural flair which became his hallmark throughout a tragically short motor racing career.

In 1973, at the age of 23, Villeneuve turned his attention to car racing, trying his hand at Formula Ford immediately after clinching the Canadian snowmobile cham-

pionship. He won seven out of ten events to take the Quebec FF title, graduating to Formula Atlantic where he had a couple of troubled seasons before hitting the headlines in 1976. He won spectacularly at the demanding Trois Rivières street circuit, beating F1 guest stars Alan Jones and James Hunt into second and third places. Hunt, then on the verge of his world championship, returned to England and advised the McLaren team to keep a firm eye on young Villeneuve.

In 1977 Villeneuve was invited to drive a third works McLaren in the British Grand Prix. He qualified an impressive ninth, splitting regular drivers Hunt (pole) and Jochen Mass (11th). Delayed by a pit stop, he ran competitively to finish tenth. Despite this superb showing McLaren opted to sign up Patrick Tambay instead. McLaren's loss was Ferrari's gain: the famous Italian team recruited Villeneuve to replace Niki Lauda at the end of the 1977 season.

Gilles quickly made himself at home in F1. It took him only until the third race of 1978, at Long Beach, to lead command-

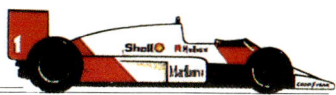

Gilles Villeneuve

Born 18 January 1952; died 8 May 1982
1977 First GP: Britain (McLaren), no pole positions, no wins, no championship points.
1978 (Ferrari) no pole positions, 1 win (Canada), 9th in world championship—17 points.
1979 (Ferrari) 1 pole position, 3 wins (South Africa, Long Beach, US East), 2nd in world championship—47 points
1980 (Ferrari) no pole positions, no wins, 10th in world champions—6 points
1981 (Ferrari) no pole positions, 2 wins (Monaco, Spain), 7th in world championship—25 points
1982 (Ferrari) 1 pole position, no wins, 15th in world championship—6 points (contested only 4 races)

Villeneuve knew from the outset that he was in a supporting role, scrupulously following in Scheckter's wheel tracks at Monza, knowing that all he had to do was disobey team orders and pass his rival to take the title for himself. That was a measure of his integrity.

The 1980 season proved a disaster for Ferrari, their cars eclipsed by far more effective ground effect rivals, notably from Williams and Ligier. But in 1981 the Italian team followed Renault down the turbo route and Villeneuve produced another two brilliant victories, in Spain and at Monaco, both in chassis that were not up to the standard of the opposition.

Throughout 1981 Villeneuve had comfortably got the measure of his teammate Didier Pironi, who stayed on with Ferrari into 1982 when, armed with a brand new car designed by Englishman Harvey Postlethwaite, prospects took a distinct upturn. However, when Pironi overtook Gilles against team orders to win the San Marino Grand Prix, in Ferrari's heartland at Imola, Gilles was incensed and never spoke to Pironi again.

Two weeks later Gilles Villeneuve crashed to his death at Zolder, colliding with a slower car that strayed into his path as he attempted to match Pironi's lap time during practice for the Belgian Grand Prix. He is still greatly missed.

ingly, but he was eliminated after an error of judgement when he tripped over a slower car he was lapping. He celebrated the end of his first full F1 season with a tremendously popular triumph in front of his home fans at Montreal. He added further wins at Long Beach, Kyalami and Watkins Glen to his total the following year, when his new teammate Jody Scheckter won the title.

Manhandling the unwieldy Ferrari 126CK through Casino Square, Villeneuve speeds to a memorable victory in the 1981 Monaco GP. He kept the pressure on Alan Jones in the closing stages, finally slipping past when the Williams developed a misfire.

THE DRIVERS

JOHN WATSON

This quiet, unobtrusive Ulsterman was a naturally gifted driver who spent much of his international career in the shadow of more famous team-mates, which should not detract from the flair which earned him a handful of outstanding victories in a ten-year full-time grand prix career.

A product of the Irish club racing scene, Watson's early enthusiasm for the sport was encouraged by his father, himself a keen amateur racer in the late 1940s. John first earned notice at the wheel of an old Lotus 48 in the 1969 Easter Monday Thruxton race where he diced expertly with established grand prix stars before sliding into a barrier. Thus encouraged, he acquired his own new Brabham and embarked on a full European F2 onslaught the following year, only to crash heavily at a race in France, breaking an arm and a leg.

He remained in F2 through 1971 and '72 before getting his F1 break in the 1973 British Grand Prix at the wheel of a private Brabham BT37. The following year he campaigned in a private Brabham BT42 for the Hexagon team, scoring his first championship point with a sixth place at Monaco. In 1975 he switched to Surtees, then on to Penske to replace the American driver Mark

Donohue, who had been killed in practice for the 1975 Austrian Grand Prix.

A year after that tragedy Watson won the 1976 Austrian Grand Prix in brilliant style at the wheel of a Penske PC4, but although he performed well throughout that season a second win eluded him. Even so, few people would have predicted that it was to be another five years before the Ulsterman would notch up his second grand prix triumph.

The Penske team withdrew from F1 at the end of 1976 and Watson switched to the Brabham-Alfa squad for the next two seasons, sustaining his speed at the front of the field, but always encountering appalling luck. An example was at Dijon in 1977 where he dominated the French Grand Prix only to run short of fuel on the last lap, allowing Mario Andretti's Lotus through to snatch victory from his grasp.

At the end of 1978, with Nelson Piquet signed to replace him at Brabham, it seemed as though Watson's F1 career might be coming to a premature end. But after the tragedy of Ronnie Peterson's death at Monza John found himself recruited to take the Swede's place at McLaren. Sadly, the once-proud British team's ground effect cars were well below par in 1979 and '80 and John became sadly demoralised, unable to come to grips with the vagaries of a succession of poor machinery.

For 1981 the team was reconstituted as McLaren International under the direction of Ron Dennis. The brilliant John Barnard designed the brand new, carbon-fibre MP4 – and Watson began to fly once again.

Below Watson leads McLaren team-mate Niki Lauda, after both had thrust their way through the field to finish 1–2 at the last F1 Long Beach GP in 1983. The McLarens had qualified in apparently hopeless 22nd and 23rd positions – but were in a different class when it came to the race.

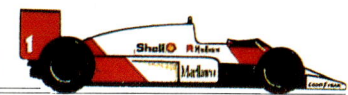

John Watson

Born 4 May 1946
1973 First GP: Britain (Brabham), no pole positions, no wins, no championship points
1974 (Brabham) no pole positions, no wins, 14th in world championship—6 points
1975 (Surtees/Penske) no pole positions, no wins, no championship points

1976 (Penske) no pole positions, 1 win (Austria), 7th in world championship—20 points
1977 (Brabham) 1 pole position, no wins, 13th in world championship—9 points
1978 (Brabham) 1 pole position, no wins, 6th in world championship—25 points
1979 (McLaren) no pole positions, no wins, 9th in world championship—15 points

1980 (McLaren) no pole positions, no wins, 10th in world championship—6 points
1981 (McLaren) no pole positions, 1 win (Britain), 6th in world championship—27 points
1982 (McLaren) no pole positions, 2 wins (Belgium, Detroit), 2nd in world championship—39 points
1983 (McLaren) no pole positions, 1 win (Long Beach), 6th in world championship—22 points

His confidence restored, he won the British Grand Prix at Silverstone, cheered to the echo by the madly enthusiastic crowd. In 1982, partnered by his old chum Niki Lauda, with whom he'd enjoyed a season at Brabham four years before, 'Wattie' won at Zolder and – brilliantly – through the streets of Detroit, keeping himself in play for the championship through to the last race, where he lost to Rosberg.

In 1983 McLaren, like Williams, were lacking a turbocharged engine, but with the Porsche-built TAG turbo in the pipeline, the future looked rosy. Even so, Watson won at Long Beach, climbing through from a qualifying position at the back of the grid, passing car after car. It was his fifth, and final, grand prix triumph.

At the end of '83 John prevaricated too long over signing a new contract. Suddenly, Alain Prost came onto the market and McLaren snapped him up. Sadly, it marked the end of the likeable Belfast driver's grand prix career.

Before perhaps his most emotional victory of all, Watson sits strapped in his McLaren MP4 during practice for the 1981 British GP. Standing, left to right, are designer John Barnard and team directors Teddy Mayer and Ron Dennis.

THIERRY BOUTSEN

This stylish Belgian driver was inspired by his compatriot Jacky Ickx in the early 1970s, and exhibits a similar polished professionalism to the former Ferrari and Porsche ace. Although Thierry enrolled in a racing school as soon as he was old enough to get a driving licence, his path to Formula 1 was strewn with pitfalls and disappointments.

In 1977, his first full season of racing – at the wheel of an elderly Formula Ford Hawke – Boutsen won 15 of his 18 races, a level of success which prompted Ickx himself to help find sponsors for his young protégé. This led him to graduate into F3 for 1979, finishing a lowly 13th in the European, but it was sufficient to earn him a place in the works Martini F3 line-up the fol-

Below Thierry Boutsen at the wheel of the Ford V6 turbo-engined Benetton B187 during the 1987 Monaco Grand Prix.

lowing year, replacing F1 graduate Alain Prost. Thierry ended the '80 season being pipped for the F3 title by Michele Alboreto.

The next rung on the ladder was Formula 2 and, after a season with a March, he joined the fledgling Spirit outfit, but was disappointed when team-mate Stefan Johansson was nominated to run their Honda-engined car in 1983. But Thierry raised sufficient sponsorship to land a seat at Arrows and drove for the Milton Keynes-based team for three and a half seasons. During that time Boutsen developed a reputation as an unflappable, smooth and reliable performer. That he was also very quick was not really demonstrated until he joined Benetton at the start of 1987.

In 1988 he finished third six times in a season dominated by the McLaren-Hondas. Switching camps again in 1989 to take over as team leader at Williams, the time is ripe for him to start winning grands prix.

MARTIN BRUNDLE

Brundle finished a glorious second at Detroit only to be later disqualified in the controversial Tyrrell 'fuel-additive' scandal.

Few drivers have taken the gamble of stepping down from F1 to consolidate their reputation, but that's what Martin Brundle did at the end of 1987. Frustrated by a dismal year with the German Zakspeed team, he reasoned that a spell with the highly competitive TWR Jaguar sports car team would better serve his long-term career interests.

Twelve months later, as world sports car champion, Brundle was restored to the grand prix elite as a member of the revitalised Brabham team, proving that the equable, even-tempered King's Lynn driver had been right to make the break.

Brundle is generally regarded as being considerably better than his machinery has allowed him to demonstrate since his grand prix debut in 1984. Born into a world of fast cars and motorsport (his father was a keen rally driver), he cut his teeth in saloon racing before switching to F3 in 1982. In the following year he battled tooth and nail for the British championship with no less a celebrity than Ayrton Senna. He lost the title to the Brazilian in the end, but that was certainly no disgrace.

Martin was signed by Ken Tyrrell at the start of 1984, finishing fifth in his first grand prix, at Rio. Later his season was blighted, first when he broke his ankles in a practice accident at Dallas, next when Tyrrell was suspended from the rest of the champion-

ship for an alleged breach of the technical regulations.

Brundle and the team were back on the scene by the start of 1985 and stayed together until the end of the following year when Martin's fourth place in the Australian GP proved the best result of his F1 career. He intends improving on that in 1989.

Above *Proving he still had the flair for F1, Martin deputised for an unwell Nigel Mansell in the 1988 Belgian GP. He was ninth past the chequered flag.*

IVAN CAPELLI

The revelation of 1988, Ivan Capelli's assurance as he raced to second place behind Alain Prost in the Portuguese Grand Prix, marked the 25-year-old Italian out as one of the brightest stars of the latest F1 generation. Moreover, Capelli's superb showing that day was certainly no flash in the pan: he had demonstrated admirable consistency and precision throughout the year and later, fleetingly, led the Japanese Grand Prix at Suzuka.

A native of Milan, Ivan won the Italian junior kart title at the age of 13 and took only another five years to graduate into Formula

Below Capelli (March 881) hounds Ayrton Senna's McLaren during the early stages of the 1988 Portuguese GP at Estoril. He would soon overtake and pull away to finish a fine second behind Prost.

3. Sixth in the 1982 Italian championship, he won that series the following year, then took the European F3 crown in 1984, winning the prestigious Monaco F3 classic for good measure.

From there Ivan's career progressed through the newly instigated Formula 3000, where he won the European championship in 1986. By then the ever-shrewd Ken Tyrrell had already given him his F1 chance, offering Capelli drives in the 1985 GP of Europe and Australian Grand Prix. He crashed in the latter, but drove superbly to finish fourth in the latter.

Briefly flirting with AGS at the end of 1986, Capelli was signed with the revitalised March team at the start of 1987 and scored another point with a fine sixth place at Monaco. At the start of 1988, armed with the superb Adrian Newey-designed March 881, Capelli quickly became a consistent force to be reckoned with, even a nasty accident at Detroit (where he broke a bone in his foot) failing to hamper his progress.

Pleasant, sensitive and gregarious, Ivan Capelli has all the attributes needed to become the first Italian world champion since Alberto Ascari.

ANDREA DE CESARIS

This Italian driver's career has been characterised by a worrying level of unpredictability. Afflicted with a disconcerting nervous facial twitch, which has always worried his rivals, de Cesaris will drive with disciplined assurance and flair, on some days, but on others with an erratic over-aggression that makes him a hazard to his fellow competitors.

Sustained in the business largely through contacts with Marlboro, the multi-national tobacco giant which has been F1's greatest benefactor over the last decade, de Cesaris started in karts before working his way through F3 and into F1. His grand prix debut was in Canada, driving an Alfa Romeo, at the tender age of 20, after which he was recruited into the McLaren International line-up for 1981.

Unfortunately Andrea's impetuosity caused a considerable number of silly accidents and there was no way he was going to be retained for '82 when Niki Lauda sig-

nalled his willingness to be lured out of retirement. He switched to Alfa Romeo, where he stayed for two seasons, scoring the best results of his career with second places in the 1983 German and South African Grands Prix. Then it was off to Ligier in 1984, only to be dropped prematurely following a massive accident during the 1985 Austrian Grand Prix.

In 1986 Andrea drove for the Italian Minardi team, with no success, before getting a break with Bernie Ecclestone's Brabham team in 1987, running alongside Riccardo Patrese. That proved yet another unproductive venture and the options seemed to have run out for de Cesaris at the end of the year. But, no, he found a berth in the new Rial team, highlighting his year with a disciplined drive to fourth place at Detroit.

In 1989 Andrea de Cesaris moves on again, joining the Italian Dallara team alongside Alex Caffi. But don't hold your breath.

In a rare cerebral moment, Andrea de Cesaris pushes his Alfa Romeo 182 into the lead of the 1982 Long Beach GP pursued by Arnoux's Renault and eventual winner Lauda's McLaren. Andrea started from pole position, but crashed....

THE DRIVERS
EDDIE CHEEVER

Highly strung and paranoid, yet immensely likable and popular, this American driver grew up in Italy where he cut his competitive teeth in kart racing during his early teens. It seemed that Eddie might be a motor racing prodigy – indeed, there were rumours that he was actually under 17 when he made his Formula 3 debut – but he has never quite scaled the heights of achievement promised by those early exploits.

Eddie made his F1 debut for the Hesketh team in a one-off outing at Kyalami in 1978, but it was not until 1980 that he became a full-time member of the grand prix set when his F2 entrant, Enzo Osella, graduated to the sport's most senior category. He spent 1981 with Tyrrell, finishing fifth in the German Grand Prix, then switched to Ligier the following year to finish second at Detroit.

In 1983 he got his big break as a member of the Renault team, alongside Alain Prost,

Eddie Cheever heads for third place, and a visit to the rostrum, at Monza during the 1988 Italian GP. He just beat his Arrows A10B team-mate Derek Warwick into fourth place.

notching up an excellent second in Canada and third in France. At the time many people were ambivalent about Prost's talent, but with the benefit of hindsight, Cheever did extremely well indeed against the French star. But he failed to retain his seat and switched to Alfa Romeo for a couple of profoundly unproductive years in 1984 and '85 and in 1986 he found himself with no drivers. The TWR Jaguar squad seemed the best available alternative and he won the Silverstone 1,000km, sharing with fellow F1 refugee Derek Warwick, later to become his team-mate with Arrows.

A one-off drive for the Haas Lola team at Detroit reminded the F1 fraternity that Cheever could still perform well and he joined the Arrows team for 1987, alongside Warwick. He managed fine fourth places in Belgium and Mexico, then stormed to an excellent third behind the Ferraris at Monza in 1988, the team's best result of the season.

TEO FABI

This serious Italian of monk-like mien has spent the last ten years alternating between F1 and racing in North America and has consolidated a strong position as Porsche Indycar works driver. His motor racing apprenticeship was served in karting, in which he shared the 1976 European championship with his brother Corrado and the late Elio de Angelis. He then graduated to front-line international racing via Formula Ford and F2, eventually moving into F1 with Toleman at the start of 1981, staying with the team until the end of the following year.

Replaced for 1983 by his compatriot Bruno Giacomelli, Fabi turned to the US-based Indycar world, taking the 1983 series by storm. He started on pole position at Indianapolis, won four races and finished runner-up in the championship behind the much more experienced Al Unser. In 1984

he started the season alternating between Indy cars and F1, eventually switching back to the grand prix scene as a full-time member of the Brabham team.

However, Fabi never achieved much in F1 despite displaying a great deal of promise. He returned to Toleman in 1985 and stayed on when the team was bought by Benetton, contesting a full programme of world championship grands prix throughout the following year. But he found himself eclipsed by Gerhard Berger and Thierry Boutsen respectively during 1986 and '87, and eventually opted for a return to Indy cars with Porsche at the start of last year.

Initial forays at the wheel of this new machine proved distinctly disappointing, but the German firm's depth of technical know-how, allied to Fabi's touch as a test driver, could pay dividends in the future.

Teo Fabi's Benetton B186, starting from pole position, leads team-mate Gerhard Berger away from the dummy grid at the start of the parade lap before the 1986 Austrian GP.

MAURICIO GUGELMIN

Mauricio Gugelmin splashes towards his first helping of Championship points with a fourth place finish in the 1988 British GP at Silverstone. Here his March hangs on ahead of the Benetton of Alessandro Nannini, who eventually beat him to third place.

An old friend of Ayrton Senna, Mauricio raced karts against his fellow Brazilian long before they became known in European motor racing circles. He started serious kart racing at the age of eight and had already won four junior championships by the time he was 12. He went on to win seven senior kart championships and the 1980 Brazilian title before graduating to cars the following year. He took the Formula Fiat title and then headed for Europe to consolidate his career.

The year after Senna had swept all before him on the British scene, Gugelmin also triumphed in the RAC FF title. Second in the 1983 FF2000 series, he triumphed in the European FF2000 contest the following year before making the inevitable move up into Formula 3. Again he matched Ayrton, winning the 1985 British championship before stepping up into Formula 3000.

With a March in 1986 and a Ralt-Honda the following year, Mauricio gained a reputation as a meticulous stylist who perhaps lacked fire and aggression. Yet his tidy technique marked him out as a man to watch and he won the 1987 Silverstone International Trophy race with flair.

March was keen to recruit a talented, intelligent and disciplined number two to Capelli in 1988, but many eyebrows were raised when they took on Gugelmin. Team manager Ian Phillips explained that they wanted a steady runner who could carry out some of the testing duties and would not disgrace himself by attempting to run too fast, too soon.

As it turned out, Gugelmin exceeded all expectations in his first F1 season, opening his points score with a brilliant fourth in the rain-soaked British Grand Prix. An affable, outgoing character, he complemented Capelli splendidly.

JEAN-PIERRE JABOUILLE

By no means one of the greatest drivers of his era, the popular Jabouille earned a glorious place in motor racing history when, at the age of 36, he won the 1979 French Grand Prix at the wheel of a Renault. Apart from the nationalistic aspects of this success, it was the first victory for a turbocharged grand prix car, opening the floodgates of turbo success which would last for another ten years.

Front-line F1 success came late, and fleetingly, to this friendly Danny Kaye lookalike. Among the first wave of drivers to rise to prominence during France's motor racing renaissance in the late 1960s, Jean Pierre Jabouille worked his way through Formula 3 at the wheel of a Matra and was a member of the French team's endurance racing line-up in the early 1970s. He was also a regular F2 contender, winning the 1976 European championship in an Elf 2, before working on early development of Renault's fledgling turbo F1 effort.

Jabouille had to suffer the brunt of the laughter as the early Renault puffed and smoked its way round the grand prix trail in 1977, but by the summer of 1978 France's national racing car was far less of a joke. Jabouille scored the marque's first championship points in the US Grand Prix before that historic victory the following summer at Dijon-Prenois.

In 1980 Jabouille stayed on with Renault, highlighting the season with a shrewd and perfectly-judged victory over Alan Jones's Williams in the Austrian Grand Prix. On the ultra-fast Osterreichring Jabouille knew he had a power advantage and drove just quickly enough to beat the world champion elect by a few lengths. Sadly, he broke a leg badly in an accident at Montreal and, although he returned to start the 1981 season at the wheel of a Ligier, he abandoned the uphill struggle after a handful of outings and retired from the cockpit.

Jean-Pierre Jabouille's second – and last – GP victory came in Austria, 1980. He held off Alan Jones's Williams by a length and is seen here on the winner's rostrum celebrating with his rival.

JEAN-PIERRE JARIER

Jean-Pierre Jarier tried reviving his F1 career with some outings for the tiny Osella team in 1981, but despite some halfway decent performances, the car seldom proved sufficiently reliable to finish any races.

Undeniably quick and naturally talented, Jean-Pierre Jarier never quite made it to the top, although there was a time in 1975 when he was strongly tipped for F1 stardom as a member of the Shadow team. Born in 1946, his grand prix career lasted over ten years, characterised by a shortage of firm results and a mere handful of championship points.

After coming to prominence at the wheel of an F3 Tecno, Jarier had his maiden F1 outing at the wheel of an outdated March in the 1971 Italian Grand Prix. But it was in F2 that he really made his name and reputation, clinching the 1973 European championship in the works March-BMW. He also had several outings for the March F1 team, but it was not until he joined Shadow in 1974 that he began to display front-running form.

Disappointingly, third place at Monaco and a fifth in Sweden were the sum total of his top six places that year, but in 1975 he qualified on pole position for both the Argentinian and Brazilian Grands Prix. In the first race his Shadow's transmission broke on the warm-up lap and he led the second in commanding style until a fuel system gremlin forced him to retire.

After leaving Shadow at the end of 1976, Jarier's career never really gelled again, despite two seasons at Tyrrell in 1979 and '80 when he reminded everybody he had the necessary speed, but not the consistency. In 1981 he switched to Osella, briefly boosting the little Italian team's prospect with his undeniable pace, but mechanical reliability eluded him.

For 1983 he was invited to join Ligier, but this proved to be an absolutely disastrous season for the French equipe with no turbo engine and a bad chassis. That was the end of Jarier's grand prix career, which had promised much but delivered little.

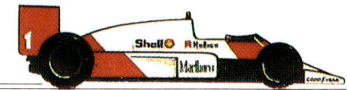

STEFAN JOHANSSON

Popular and cheerful, this Swede had all the appropriate racing credentials when he finally graduated into F1 with the aspiring Spirit-Honda team in the summer of 1973. A successful kartist, winner of the British F3 championship in 1979 and a Formula 2 pace-setter, Johansson was quick, brave and talented. He was also immensely unlucky and, despite spells with Ferrari and McLaren, his maiden grand prix victory still eluded him at the beginning of 1989.

When Honda switched their engine supply contract to Williams for 1984, Johansson filled in as best he could, accepting guest drives with both Tyrrell and Toleman. In the Italian Grand Prix he brought the Toleman home a fine fourth, securing a contract as their number one driver for the following seasons, taking over from Ayrton Senna.

Just when it seemed that Johansson stood on the threshold of success, lack of a tyre contract prompted Toleman to shelve their programme temporarily, and Stefan's ambitions looked as though they might be thwarted. But René Arnoux was dropped from the Ferrari line-up after a single race and Johansson took his place.

Running competitively in 1985, Stefan finished a strong second in both the Canadian and Detroit Grands Prix, firming up a reputation which kept him in the Maranello squad for 1986. But Ferrari's competitiveness waned dramatically and Stefan seemed beset by a succession of mechanical problems and sheer bloody bad luck as he wrestled his way through to the end of that second year.

Ferrari dropped him in favour of Gerhard Berger, but he picked up the prestige number two McLaren ride alongside Alain Prost, only to be replaced by Ayrton Senna after a year. He was fortunate not to sink without trace after a dismal season driving a hopeless Ligier in 1988.

Stefan Johansson kerb-hops his Ferrari towards third place in the 1986 Australian GP, his last outing for the Italian team. He enjoyed a season at McLaren in 1987 before his fortunes faded.

123

ALESSANDRO NANNINI

With Thierry Boutsen's departure to Williams, Alessandro Nannini faced the 1989 season as team leader at Benetton, backed up by rising English star Johnny Herbert. This promised to be an enormous challenge and responsibility for the popular, chain-smoking Italian who claims that with his sister Gianna firmly established as one of his country's leading rock singers, he is never likely to become the most famous member of the Nannini family.

Sandro probably does himself less than credit. In 1988, after two years of struggling with an uncompetitive Minardi, he received a long-overdue reward when he was promoted to the Benetton-Ford line-up. More significantly, he fully justified the team's faith by producing a succession of mature drives, the most outstanding a third place at rain-soaked Silverstone and a chase through to ninth at Monza after losing a lap at the start with mechanical problems.

After cutting his competitive teeth in rally-ing with a Citroen Dyane, rather an unusual choice of car, Alessandro quickly graduated to the cockpit of a Lancia Stratos, something of an F1 car to the rally fraternity throughout much of the 1970s. In 1980 he went circuit racing in Formula Fiat Abarth, vaulting directly into F2 with Minardi at the start of 1982.

His 1983 and '84 seasons were beset by a sequence of mechanical breakdowns and his plans to switch to F1 were thwarted in 1985 when the sport's governing body decreed that he had insufficient F2 results to earn a super licence. But he kept his career afloat with a fourth season driving Lancia sports cars before making the step up in 1986.

Two years with Minardi did not produce hard results, but he enhanced his reputation by pushing the unwieldy machine further up the grid than it deserved. Cast in the same mould as Capelli, he has star quality in abundance.

Alessandro Nannini hounds Nelson Piquet's Lotus for third place during the 1988 San Marino GP. The Italian later had a spin and eventually finished sixth.

JONATHAN PALMER

Left *Jonathan Palmer has struggled with a series of less-than-competitive cars for much of his F1 career, but he scored his first championship points with a fine fifth at Monaco in this Tyrrell. His outings for Zakspeed (below) he would prefer to forget.*

Jonathan Palmer's level-headed pragmatism is reflected by the fact that he completed his training and qualified as a doctor before opting for a full-time career in professional motor racing. Born in 1957, he qualified in 1978 and held two hospital posts before relinquishing his medical aspirations.

He began his racing at the wheel of an Austin-Healey sports car before deciding that motor racing would be his long-term ambition, subsequently switching to Formula Ford, the nursery for future F1 talent. In 1981 he won one of the coveted Grovewood Awards presented to young drivers who display outstanding promise, and then set himself on the path to international recognition with victory in the 1982 British F3 Championship.

F2 followed with the Ralt-Honda squad and Palmer duly emerged as European Champion, being rewarded with a one-off drive in a third Williams in the 1983 Grand Prix of Europe. He graduated full-time to F1 with the RAM team in 1984, but this and the German Zakspeed organisation, for whom he drove in 1985 and '86, were small and moderately financed teams. Nonetheless Jonathan quickly gained a reputation as a cool and methodical racer whose orderly mind and clear sighted approach helped him develop into a fine test and development driver.

At the end of 1986 he took a major gam-

ble in holding out for the second McLaren drive which eventually went to Stefan Johansson. For a few weeks it seemed as though Jonathan might have been left out in the wilderness, but he was rescued by Ken Tyrrell and restored his reputation in 1987, winning the Jim Clark Trophy for drivers of normally aspirated cars.

In 1988 he remained with Tyrrell, battling gallantly against the odds in a seriously uncompetitive car. However, he stays with Tyrrell for 1989 and relishes the chance of being measured against his new team-mate, former Ferrari driver Michele Alboreto.

THE DRIVERS

RICCARDO PATRESE

One-time *enfant terrible* of the grand prix set, Patrese is nowadays generally a steadier performer than he was during his formative years in F1. He drove his first championship race at Monaco in 1977 at the age of 24, having by then gained considerable racing experience in F3 and F2. But to many people Riccardo seemed over-confident, too frequently wearing a supercilious smirk on his lips. Moreover, too frequently, he seemed to get himself tangled up in controversial episodes out on the circuit.

taking part in the United States GP as a punishment. Looking back, it was a shameful deed and Patrese was seriously wronged on that occasion.

Switching to Brabham for 1982, he finally scored his maiden grand prix win at Monaco, five years to the day after his debut. The following season he won the South African Grand Prix at Kyalami, since when victory has failed to come his way again. His career then took him to Alfa Romeo (1984-5) then back to Brabham

Riccardo Patrese leads the 1981 Long Beach GP in his Arrows ahead of Carlos Reutemann's Williams.

After running his first season with Shadow, he switched to the newly established Arrows squad the following year, displaying considerable potential and confidence. Sadly, he was blamed in some quarters as having triggered off the multiple startline pile up at Monza that year which resulted in the death of Ronnie Peterson. He was later absolved of blame, but the other drivers held what amounted to a disgraceful 'kangaroo court', linking up to ban Patrese from

(1986-7), before Frank Williams signed him up to partner Nigel Mansell in 1988. That latter decision surprised everybody, for although Patrese is a capable driver, he tends only to pull out all the stops when a decent result is at stake.

Patrese's participation in the 1988 Australian Grand Prix equals Graham Hill's achievement of 176 GP starts, so the 35-year old Italian stands poised to break that record in 1989.

PATRICK TAMBAY

Left Patrick Tambay had the tough task of replacing Villeneuve at Ferrari after Gilles' death in 1982.

Popularly regarded as the Prince Charming of Formula 1 during his time in the sport's most exalted category, this debonair, stylish and courteous Frenchman was another driver who never quite earned the rewards his talent deserved. The cosmopolitan Tambay was educated in France and the United States, speaks fluent English and was a talented downhill ski racer before motor racing caught his eye at the end of 1971.

At the Paul Ricard driving school he won the Volant Elf scholarship (the year before Didier Pironi) and, after two seasons in Formula Renault, bypassed F3 and moved directly into the European F2 championship arena. In the next couple of seasons he sampled Can-Am sports cars in North America before his F2 exploits earned him an F1 chance at the wheel of an Ensign entered by wealthy Hong Kong enthusiast Teddy Yip in the 1977 British Grand Prix. Scoring five championship points in his first six grands prix, Patrick earned a place in the McLaren line-up for 1978, partnering James Hunt.

Sadly, McLaren by then were losing their competitive pace as rival teams' ground effect chassis outclassed their machines, so Tambay had two lean seasons before being replaced by Alain Prost at the start of 1980. As something of a consolation prize he returned to the USA, won the Can-Am and found a way back to F1 the following year thanks to the philanthropic Teddy Yip and his tiny Theodore team.

When Jean-Pierre Jabouille retired from the Ligier squad Tambay took his place, but was dropped at the end of the season. His next F1 chance came in the tragic aftermath of Gilles Villeneuve's death when he was recruited by Ferrari. But he earned his spurs by winning the German Grand Prix the day after Didier Pironi was so crucially injured. In '83 he scored a precious victory in front of the Ferrari fans at Imola. His stints with the Renault and Haas-Lola teams never offered the machinery to scale such peaks of achievement again.

Above Patrick Tambay started from pole position in the 1983 Austrian GP, leading comfortably in the opening stages of the race. Team-mate Arnoux then outfumbled him to take the lead, Patrick later retiring.

DEREK WARWICK

Warwick holds second place at the wheel of the Toleman TG181B in the 1982 British Grand Prix. He retired — officially owing to driveshaft failure, although many observers believed he was running on only half-tanks.

At the start of 1984 Derek Warwick was tipped for stardom as Britian's next grand prix ace. Succeeding Alain Prost at Renault, he at last had the equipment to run consistently at the front of the field. In discussion of sheer talent and determination in the F1 paddocks of the world, Derek Warwick's name comes up time and again. Since those fleeting halcyon days with Renault in '84 when victory seemed just around the corner, Warwick has continued to hammer on the doors of success with a ferocity and determination which is every bit the equal of his (now) more famous colleague and rival Nigel Mansell. Moreover, Warwick's universally sunny disposition make him enormously popular in a business where ego can be a destructive force.

Encouraged by his father and uncle, who run the family trailer-building business in rural Hampshire, Derek was a stock-car champion on dirt ovals when little more than a child. He graduated through the rough and tumble of Formula Ford through to F3, all the time financed by his family, and triumphed in one of the British F3 championships in 1978, racing competitively against Nelson Piquet.

He moved up into F2 where he forged a bond with the Toleman team, spearheading their ambitious graduation to F1 at the start of 1981. He then switched to Renault in '84, only to see the team's fortunes plunge in 1985 and the French company withdraw from F1. He returned to F1 with Brabham after the death of Elio de Angelis, then in 1987 switched to Arrows, where he has stayed. A devoted family man who lives in Jersey, Warwick remains determined to lay the ghosts of his past misfortune and claw his way to the winner's circle before he calls it a day.

STARS OF THE FUTURE

At the start of the 1989 season there were several new young talents poised on the verge of grand prix success and a handful more waiting in the wings amongst the junior categories. One of Britain's bright young hopes, 24-year old Johnny Herbert, moved into front-line F1 at the wheel of a Benetton-Ford as partner to Alessandro Nannini. The winner of the 1987 British F3 title, Herbert's determined recovery from serious injury when he crashed his Formula 3000 Reynard at Brands Hatch in August 1988 suggests this youngster has the necessary tenacity to go with his undoubted natural skill.

Others to watch out for include 1987 European F3000 champion Roberto Moreno, a young Brazilian who has hovered on the fringes of F1 for several seasons. In 1988 he gained valuable experience as Ferrari's F1 test driver, doing a considerable amount of development work with the new naturally-aspirated 3.5-litre V12 engine, and was signed to drive a full programme of races for the Italian Coloni team in 1989.

Italy's Stefano Modena, who preceded Moreno as F3000 title holder, should consolidate a growing reputation in the revived Brabham team; while France's Yannick Dalmas shows considerable promise, although an attack of Legionnaire's disease was a major set-back at the end of 1988.

Looking further ahead, Keke Rosberg's gifted new Finnish contemporary 'J.J.' Lehto, winner of the 1988 British F3 title, promises to sustain his country's reputation in the world championship arena, while fellow Finn Mika Hakknnen and Scotland's Allan McNish have marked themselves out as youngsters to watch, though barely out of their teens.

Below, left Stefano Modena, 1987 European F3000 Champion, proved his F1 quality by finishing third in the 1989 Monaco GP.

Below, right Johnny Herbert made a sensational F1 debut for Benetton in the 1989 Brazilian GP. He finished fourth, close behind Alain Prost's McLaren and Mauricio Gugelmin's March.

THE HONOURS

FORMULA I WORLD CHAMPIONSHIP

THE HONOURS

1979

Scheckter takes the title: Jones makes his mark for Williams: Renault get on the winning map

Preceding two pages
*Ayrton Senna (left) and
Alain Prost dominated 1988
for McLaren, with the rest
scrambling for the minor
places. Sharing the rostrum
here at Paul Ricard was
third-placed Michele
Alboreto (Ferrari).*

*Right Jacques Laffite heads
for victory in Argentina at
the wheel of the Cosworth-
engined Ligier JS11. He won
again in Brazil to take an
early lead in the
Championship, but the
French team's fortunes
faded thereafter.*

The 1979 world championship season opened amid much fascination and expectancy, grand prix racing having arrived at an historic turning point the previous year with the success of the sensational ground-effect Lotus 79 which carried Mario Andretti majestically to title victory. Colin Chapman's mastery of under-car aerodynamics rewrote the parameters of grand prix car performance at a stroke. The opposition had to follow the same path or face competitive oblivion.

As the cars were unloaded in Argentina for the first race of the year, it was difficult to foresee that Lotus stood to be eclipsed by their rivals' second-generation ground-effect challengers. Less difficult to prophesy, however, was the Renault team's burgeoning form. Since the French turbo's race debut in the summer of 1977, they had made enormous progress with a trend-setting power unit which also changed the whole complexion of F1 over the following decade. Less obvious and difficult to quantify were the challenges offered by Ferrari, who had signed Jody Scheckter to partner Gilles Villeneuve, and Williams. Neither of these teams had their 1979 cars ready for the two South American races and were relying on the '78 machines for the time being.

Newly recruited by team Lotus, the moody, sometimes brilliant Argentinian Carlos Reutemann hoped to win his home grand prix at last, at the wheel of the ground-effect type 79. He was surprised to wind up third on the starting grid, behind the debutant Ligier JS11s of Frenchman Jacques Laffite and Patrick Depailler. A first corner multiple pile-up, subsequently blamed on McLaren driver John Watson, meant the race had to be restarted, but Laffite had an easy time, waltzing away into the distance and winning as he pleased. An ill-timed pit stop, made in the vain hope of saving a slight fuel vapourisation problem, lost Depailler the chance to make it a Ligier 1-2. As it was, he finished fourth behind Reutemann and Watson, in a McLaren M28, both of whom were shocked to discover that their machinery was not up to the competitive level that would be required in 1979.

Further back, world champion Andretti was a dejected and lapped fifth ahead of Emerson Fittipaldi's Copersucar-Fittipaldi, and 19-year old debutant Elio de Angelis did well to finish seventh in his Shadow DN9.

A fortnight later, at São Paulo's spectacular Interlagos circuit, Laffite and Depailler left their opposition behind to finish the race in a commanding 1-2 for Ligier. Reutemann was left trailing third this time, with French-

1979 DRIVERS' CHAMPIONSHIP

		points
1	Jody Scheckter	51
2	Gilles Villeneuve	47
3	Alan Jones	40
4	Jacques Laffite	36
5	Clay Regazzoni	29
6	Patrick Depailler	20
	Carlos Reutemann	20
8	René Arnoux	17
9	John Watson	15
10	Jean-Pierre Jarier	14
	Didier Pironi	14
	Mario Andretti	14
13	Jean-Pierre Jabouille	9
14	Niki Lauda	4
15	Nelson Piquet	3
	Elio de Angelis	3
	Jochen Mass	3
	Jacky Ickx	3
19	Riccardo Patrese	2
	Hans Stuck	2
21	Emerson Fittipaldi	1

CONSTRUCTORS' CHAMPIONSHIP

		points
1	FERRARI	113
2	WILLIAMS	75
3	LIGIER	61
4	LOTUS	39
5	TYRRELL	28
6	RENAULT	26
7	McLAREN	15
8	BRABHAM	7
9	ARROWS	5
10	SHADOW	3
11	ATS	2
12	FITTIPALDI	1

man Didier Pironi fourth in a new Tyrrell 009, which was so similar to the Lotus 79 that most observers could only tell them apart by their colours. Fifth and sixth were Villeneuve and Scheckter's ageing Ferrari 312T3s: Maranello's Michelin-shod machines were clearly outclassed.

There was a surprise in store for their rivals when the grand prix circuit reconvened to do battle at Johannesburg's Kyalami circuit a month later, however. The South African Grand Prix was the debut of the functional, yet highly effective, Ferrari 312T4. Designed by the Italian team's brilliant, if temperamental, chief engineer Mauro Forghieri, it was to prove Maranello's best-ever effort at producing a competitive ground-effect challenger. Hamstrung by the width of its flat-12-cylinder engine, the T4 had smaller ground-effect side pods than its rivals who used the compact Ford-Cosworth V8, but a combination of clever engineering, powerful engine, Michelin tyres and two highly motivated drivers made it a formidable contender throughout the rest of the year.

The new Ferraris qualified second and third, but the pole position provided a real surprise. Benefiting from the turbo's sustained power ouput in the thinner air at Kyalami's 5000ft altitude, Jean-Pierre Jabouille qualified the Renault in first place. Moreover, since the French team was not yet using its ground-effect chassis, this performance was indisputably owed to engine power.

Above Gilles Villeneuve's Ferrari 312T4 laps Riccardo Patrese's Arrows en route to victory in the Long Beach Grand Prix. But it was his team-mate Jody Scheckter (*right*), seen winning at Monaco, who emerged with the drivers' crown.

with Villeneuve closing fast, himself gambled on a late-race stop for fresh rubber. But the French Canadian rising star had everything under control, beating his ostensible team leader by just under four seconds. Jean-Pierre Jarier's Tyrrell wound up third ahead of the Lotus twins and Andretti and Reutemann were fourth and fifth. Niki Lauda came sixth in his new Brabham BT48, the Alfa Romeo V12 engine of which had been built in record time over the winter specifically to fit a more efficient ground effect chassis.

Back across the Atlantic in California, Villeneuve and Scheckter produced the same result in the Long Beach Grand Prix, their Ferrari T4s riding the bumps and ripples of the coastal street circuit with a speed and durability that depressed their opposition. However, the first signs that the Prancing Horse would not steamroller the championship could be gauged from the storming drive to third place by Alan Jones in the previous year's Williams FW06. The British team's opposition was also treated to a pit lane preview of the new ground effect Williams FW07 which did not race, having been brought to California only for post-race tests at Ontario Motor Speedway.

The Spanish Grand Prix opened the European season at Madrid's tortuous Jarama circuit, and this fourth round of the title chase put Ligier back on top. Laffite and Depailler qualified 1-2 and then staged a private race for the lead, Patrick taking the win after

Villeneuve and Scheckter gamble

Jabouille briefly led at the start, but the race was halted when Kyalami was soaked by torrential rain after a couple of laps. At the second start, with the circuit still soaking, Villeneuve started on rain tyres, while local hero Scheckter gambled on using slicks. Sure enough, the track surface dried out, and when Villeneuve made his inevitable stop to change tyres at the end of lap 15, Jody surged into the lead.

Sadly, Scheckter then ran too hard and,

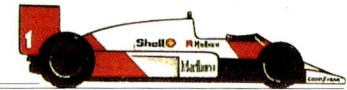

Jacques fumbled a gear change and over-revved his engine. Reutemann wound up second in the old Lotus 79, with Andretti third in his first drive in the complex Lotus 80, which featured a system of aerodynamic sliding skirts running almost the full length of the car. Scheckter was a lonely fourth ahead of both Tyrrells, while a pair of new Williams FW07s made unobtrusive race debuts, starting in the middle of the grid, before retiring with gear-selection problems (Jones) and engine failure (Clay Regazzoni).

Jones makes his mark

The new challenger from Frank Williams' Didcot factory did not take long to assert itself as a potential winner. In the Belgian Grand Prix at Zolder Jones was among the two Ligiers, battling for the lead, finally gaining the upper hand to pull away from the French cars. Sadly, a minor electrical fault thwarted the Australian's fine effort and Scheckter, picking up the pace superbly, came through to win ahead from Laffite and Pironi's Tyrrell. Villeneuve tangled with Regazzoni's Williams on the opening lap and spent the rest of the afternoon heroically recovering to third — before running short of

fuel on the last lap, dropping to a disappointing seventh. It was a success that hoisted Scheckter into the world championship points lead, which he maintained through to the end of the season.

Not that Villeneuve was going to give up without a fight, of course. The two Ferraris buttoned up the front row at Monaco where Jody led throughout for his second win of the season, while Villeneuve broke his transmission. Jones held third with the new Williams, only to damage his suspension against a guard rail, leaving team-mate Regazzoni to finish a close second. Reutemann was third ahead of John Watson's McLaren M28, the Ulsterman's first sunny moment in an otherwise brutally disappointing season grappling with a totally uncompetitive car.

During the month-long break that followed before the French Grand Prix, former world champion James Hunt announced his retirement from the Wolf team and Depailler was badly injured in a hang-gliding accident. Their places were taken by Jacky Ickx and Keke Rosberg respectively, but neither were among the leading bunch at Dijon-Prenois, where Jabouille sailed confidently to an historic win at the wheel of the superbly effective Renault RS11. Second place was the focus of an heroic wheel-banging battle between Arnoux's Renault

Early in the Belgian Grand Prix at Zolder, Patrick Depailler's Ligier heads Jones's Williams, Piquet's Brabham, Laffite's Ligier, Andretti's Lotus, Regazzoni's Williams and the Ferraris of Scheckter and Villeneuve.

The 1979 season saw the retirement of James Hunt after a handful of races in this Wolf WR8. The former World Champion confessed he'd lost his taste for the business and considered the risks no longer worthwhile.

and Villeneuve's Ferrari, Gilles just getting the verdict, with Alan Jones pounding home fourth, the best-placed of the Goodyear runners.

Frank Williams's team was now not so much knocking on the door of success as on the verge of beating it down. So when Alan Jones vanished into the distance from the start of the British Grand Prix at Silverstone, it looked like being Frank's great moment. It was, but that memorable win was scored not by Jones, but by Regazzoni. Alan's FW07 suffered a fractured water pump and overheated its way into retirement, leaving the veteran 39-year old Swiss with what was the final victory of an illustrious career. Arnoux's Renault and Jarier's Tyrrell were second and third, with John Watson's brand new – and much improved – McLaren M29 outfumbling Scheckter to take fourth on the very last lap.

Jones had to wait only another fortnight to score the second grand prix win of his career (the first had been in Austria in 1977 at the wheel of a Shadow) when he led Regazzoni home for a Williams 1-2 at Hockenheim. He was lucky, grappling with a deflating rear tyre in the closing stages, allowing Clay to get uncomfortably close. Laffite, Watson and Scheckter were next up, the Ligier driver displacing Villeneuve from second place in the championship points table.

Jones was too far back to pose a realistic title threat, but another win in Austria, comfortably from Villeneuve, moved him back into fourth place in the points table.

Villeneuve was second in the race from Laffite and Scheckter, re-taking his runner's-up slot in the overall rankings. It was getting a bit too tight for Scheckter's comfort, but the South African kept his nerve admirably, knowing that even if he counldn't match his zestful young team-mate for speed, he was likely to make fewer mistakes.

That premise was underlined graphically in the Dutch Grand Prix at Zandvoort, the seaside circuit now modified with a chicane to slow the cars on its fastest section. Scheckter and Villeneuve qualified side-by-side on row three, but while Gilles burst away at the start to challenge Jones's Williams for the lead, Jody overheated his clutch and dropped almost to last before it began to bite properly. While Villeneuve became embroiled in a ferocious scrap with the Australian's Williams, Scheckter got down to the business of making up ground.

The afternoon ended with Villeneuve taking the lead, losing it again with a wild spin that signalled an imminent tyre deflation, before finally flying off the road when the over-heating Michelin finally disintegrated. Unbowed, the indomitable Canadian drove the crippled car back to the pits on three wheels, virtually wrecking it in the process. Jones won, and Scheckter finished second.

Laffite clung to his increasingly frail title hopes with third place, while a fourth place gave Nelson Piquet his first championship points, the young Brazilian F3 graduate bringing the surviving Brabham-Alfa home a lap behind the winner.

Jody's clincher

To win the championship Scheckter now had to win at Monza, in front of Ferrari's home crowd. It had been four years since Maranello scored a home success in the Italian Grand Prix, but Jody performed perfectly, leading Villeneuve all the way to a memorable 1-2 finish. Gilles behaved in suitably honourable fashion (although he later confessed that he was praying that Scheckter's car would fail), playing second fiddle as requested, even though he could have kept his own title hopes open by passing Jody. Jones wound up a disappointing ninth after an early stop for a new battery, Laffite's engine blew up and it was Regazzoni who finished third, having survived a second-lap collision with Piquet. The Brazilian was lucky to escape as his Brabham was ripped in two with the engine and chassis landing on opposite sides of the track.

The championship settled, Villeneuve was off the leash in front of his home crowd at Montreal, embroiled in a ferocious battle with Jones's more competitive Williams. First Alan led, then Gilles, then Alan, and the Williams just scrambled past the chequered flag first with a second in hand over the Ferrari. Regazzoni was third from Scheckter, but the real news happened off the circuit. Although Niki Lauda had a brand new Cosworth-engined Brabham BT49 for the first time, the season-long struggle with the troublesome Brabham-Alfa has taken its toll on him. He pulled into the pits mid-way through first practice, took team boss Bernie Ecclestone to one side and announced that he was retiring there and then. By the evening he had slipped away to the McDonnell-Douglas factory in California to discuss delivery of a new plane for his expanding airline LaudaAir. But, almost three years later, he would be back.

The season was rounded off with Villeneuve displaying his masterly car control yet again, splashing off into the distance at Watkins Glen to lead the United States Grand Prix, but as the track began to dry out Jones's Williams closed in and eventually took the lead on lap 32 when Gilles stopped for slicks. Four laps later the leading Williams stopped, but in a slightly fumbled tyre change, one of the wheel securing nuts was not torqued up properly. Jones lasted less than another lap before he found himself at the wheel of an FW07 tricycle, happily slithering to a halt without any damage.

Arnoux finished second for Renault ahead of Pironi's Tyrrell and two new points scorers, de Angelis in the Shadow and Hans-Joachim Stuck, son of the great pre-war Auto Union ace, in at ATS. Rounding off the top half-dozen was John Watson at the end of a bitterly disappointing first season with McLaren in which the machinery just hadn't allowed him to compete with Ferrari, Ligier or Williams. Things were to get worse for the popular Ulsterman before they got better.

John Watson finished fourth in the British GP, helping to swing McLaren fortunes in the right direction on the maiden outing of the new M29, which had been rushed through to completion after the M28 proved uncompetitive.

THE HONOURS

1980

Jones takes Williams to the title: Piquet stars for Brabham: Ferrari fade: Controversy over future regulations

The 1980 world championship season was played out against the background of a complex pseudo-political battle between the sport's governing body, the Fédération Internationale du Sport Automobile (FISA), under the presidency of the volatile Jean-Marie Balestre, and the Formula One Constructors' Association (FOCA), a predominantly British cartel of team owners guided by shrewd Brabham team boss Bernie Ecclestone.

The dispute centred on who was to run motor racing, a professional sport that had developed into a lucrative and extremely prestigious international business. Balestre felt that FISA had rather lost its grip in recent years, with much of the initiative taken by Ecclestone and his colleagues, who negotiated package contracts for races and television coverage from a position of strength.

Nelson Piquet scrambles his Brabham BT49 through into the lead in the Long Beach GP, taking an advantage he was never to lose. He is pursued by René Arnoux's Renault and the Alfa Romeo of Bruno Giacomelli.

1980 DRIVERS' CHAMPIONSHIP

		points
1	Alan Jones	67
2	Nelson Piquet	54
3	Carlos Reutemann	42
4	Jacques Laffite	34
5	Didier Pironi	32
6	René Arnoux	29
7	Elio de Angelis	13
8	Jean-Pierre Jabouille	9
9	Riccardo Patrese	7
10	Derek Daly	6
	Jean-Pierre Jarier	6
	Keke Rosberg	6
	Gilles Villeneuve	6
	John Watson	6
15	Emerson Fittipaldi	5
	Alain Prost	5
17	Bruno Giacomelli	4
	Jochen Mass	4
19	Jody Scheckter	2
20	Hector Rebaque	1
	Mario Andretti	1
	Patrick Gaillard	1

CONSTRUCTORS' CHAMPIONSHIP

		points
1	WILLIAMS	120
2	LIGIER	66
3	BRABHAM	55
4	RENAULT	38
5	LOTUS	14
6	TYRRELL	12
7	ARROWS	11
	FITTIPALDI	11
	McLAREN	11
10	FERRARI	8
11	ALFA ROMEO	4

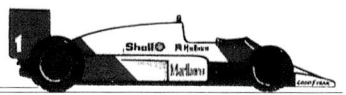

He was determined to restore FISA as the ultimate power in racing, backed by teams such as Ferrari (Fiat), Renault and Alfa-Romeo, all of which had a strong car-manufacturing base and were active in other areas of the sport.

At the end of 1979 Balestre intervened in the rule-making process when FISA decreed that sliding skirts, the aerodynamic devices essential to ground-effect efficiency, would be banned from the start of 1981. That set him on course for a head-on collision with FOCA, whose members' relied on ingenuity of chassis design to counter the imminent threat from the more powerful turbo brigade. Formula 1 thus entered a painful period of transition during which a series of ructions threatened to tear the business asunder, with the real possibility of two separate championships being run for the two opposing factions.

There were changes of drivers in several teams for the new season. Reutemann switched from Lotus to partner Jones at Williams, so Regazzoni moved on to the tiny Ensign line-up and de Angelis went to Lotus. Patrick Tambay was replaced at McLaren by young French F3 star Alain Prost while Depailler, struggling to recover from leg injuries, joined Alfa Romeo with Bruno Giacomelli, leaving Pironi to take his place alongside Laffite at Ligier. Ireland's Derek Daly joined Jarier at Tyrrell, and Argentinian Ricardo Zunino partnered Piquet in the Brabham line-up.

Jones sustained his 1979 momentum when the year started at Beunos Aires, beating Piquet into second place in a searing Argentine Grand Prix, while Keke Rosberg, driving for the Fittipaldi team which had absorbed the Wolf Racing outfit over the winter, underlined his long-term potential with a fine third. Derek Daly, Giacomelli and new boy Prost completed the top half dozen, the young Alain already demonstrating the flair that would eventually earn him world championship glory.

Originally scheduled for the bland Jacarepaguá circuit at Rio de Janeiro (its venue in 1978), the Brazilian Grand Prix reverted to Interlagos when it became clear that the Rio track needed resurfacing. René Arnoux signalled the Renault team's long-term intentions with an almost unchallenged victory over de Angelis, with Jones trailing home third after a self-confessedly unsatisfactory performance.

At high-altitude Kyalami, Renault pretty much had the South African Grand Prix to itself, Arnoux triumphing for a second time

after Jabouille succumbed to a deflated tyre. Jones gave them a run for their money, but retired with gearbox trouble, leaving Laffite and Pironi second and third for Ligier ahead of Piquet's Brabham. With two wins in three races, Arnoux led the title chase by five points.

Promotion to team leader rested easily on Piquet's shoulders and he rose to the occasion at Long Beach, qualifying his Brabham BT49 on pole position and leading all the way, aided by Jones spending the first few laps bottled up behind Depailler's Alfa: by the time he got through to second place, Piquet had vanished into the distance. The Australian was eventually eliminated in a collision with Giacomelli's Alfa, so Patrese's Arrows inherited third from Fittipaldi and Watson, with world champion Scheckter a distant fifth. Ferrari's revamped 312T5 proved hopelessly uncompetitive throughout 1980 as Maranello concentrated its efforts on long-term development of a new 1.5-litre turbocharged contender. Sadly the race was marred by a serious accident when Clay Regazzoni crashed the Ensign, suffering back injuries which left him paralysed.

At Zolder for the Belgian Grand Prix Jones confidently planted his Williams FW07B on pole position, but Pironi's Ligier imme-

Alan Jones opens his World Championship assault with a splendid victory in the Argentine GP at Buenos Aires, achieved in sweltering heat on a crumbling track.

Mechanics keep themselves amused at Jarama while, behind the scenes, political wrangling over the status of the Spanish GP continues.

diately took the initiative at the start. The Frenchman was in superb form, never putting a wheel wrong all the way to his first grand prix victory, leaving Jones trailing a distant second. Laffite's Ligier wound up third with Reutemann fourth in the other Williams.

Clearly, if Ligier could sustain their reliability, Pironi would be a threat to Jones's title aspirations. They rejoined the battle together at Monaco where trouble brewed before practice, with some drivers who were concerned about the safety of allowing 27 cars out in a free-for-all qualifying session threatening a boycott.

The trouble thankfully subsided and Didier this time started from pole position with Reutemann second on the grid and Jones third. The Ligier got away first, with Alan getting the jump on his team-mate, and the two of them disappeared, running nose to tail. But Jones's differential failed and Pironi glanced a guard rail in Casino Square, leaving the stealthy Reutemann an easy run to his sole victory that season.

Laffite wound up second from Piquet, with Jochen Mass's Arrows fourth and the heroic Villeneuve wrestling his way to an eventual fifth in his recalcitrant Ferrari. A spectacular multiple shunt at the first corner on the opening lap eliminated Prost, Giacomelli and Tyrrell team-mates Daly and Jarier. The Irishman's car was launched high into the air over the heads of his rivals but, fortunately, they were all unhurt.

These were minor problems compared with the controversy which erupted before the Spanish Grand Prix at Jarama. Earlier in the season FISA president Balestre had introduced mandatory pre-race briefings and several drivers were fined for not attending

at Zolder and Monaco. Now Balestre said that the offending drivers would not be permitted to race in Spain unless the fines were paid.

FOCA responded by threatening that their members wouldn't race unless the fines were quashed. The organisers attempted to circumvent the problem by altering the sanctioning arrangements under which the event was run, with the result that the event effectively became a 'pirate' race outside FISA jurisdiction.

At this point Ferrari, Renault and Alfa Romeo opted out, so the race went ahead as an all-FOCA affair with Reutemann leading from the start and Laffite soon nipping past Jones to take up the challenge from second place. On lap 36 local novice Emilio de Villota, ironically at the wheel of a private ex-works Williams, grabbed the headlines in the local papers by eliminating both Carlos and Jacques as they lapped him, allowing a chuckling Jones through to score another victory. Mass, de Angelis and Jarier followed him across the line, but it profited them little. FISA decreed that the race had no valid status and no championship points were awarded.

Jones's two in a row

The season was now polarising, somewhat unpleasantly, between the French and the British, so when Alan Jones out-ran both Ligiers to win the French Grand Prix at Paul Ricard there was considerable glee within the Williams camp. More importantly, Alan took the championship points lead from Piquet with his win, consolidating it with an

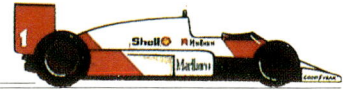

equally impressive success in the British Grand Prix at Brands Hatch.

For a time it looked as though Pironi and Laffite might turn the tables on Williams's home soil. The JS11s proved blindingly fast in practice and comfortably out-ran Jones in the opening stages. But both the French machines suffered problems with leaking wheel rims, which made their tyres deflate. In Laffite's case, this caused an enormous accident at Hawthorn Hill from which the Frenchman was lucky to emerge unscathed. Their demise left Jones to lead home Piquet, Reutemann and the Tyrrells to strengthen his grasp on the title. Completing the top half dozen at Brands Hatch to consolidate his fast-rising reputation, Alain Prost was doing a good job of humbling his more experienced team-mate John Watson. The Ulsterman was finding it very difficult to adapt his technique to get the best out of ground effect machinery, and had even ignominiously failed to qualify at Monaco. Yet, as Prost was to recall many years later, he remained unstintingly helpful to his young French colleague and never displayed any envy over his rapid rise to prominence.

Over at Lotus, meanwhile, the Andretti/Chapman love affair was most certainly coming to a close. Two years earlier the Lotus boss had likened his relationship with Mario to the one he had enjoyed with the late Jim Clark, but the strain of two seasons with uncompetitive machinery was taking its toll. Coming away from Brands Hatch, Mario still had no points, despite the unloved Lotus 80 having been shelved and replaced with the more conventional type 81 for the start of the 1980 season.

The F1 fraternity lost one of its most popular members before the German Grand Prix at Hockenheim: testing his Alfa Romeo at the track nine days before the race Patrick Depailler was killed in a high-speed accident. It was discovered later that crucial catch fencing, which might have cushioned the terrible impact, had not been erected in time for the test. Understandably the grand prix was run in a depressed atmosphere with only one Alfa present for Giacomelli, the team's second driver.

This very fast circuit suited Renault admirably and Jean-Pierre Jabouille powered into the lead from the start, pursued by Jones. At two-thirds distance the French turbo retired with engine failure, so Jones looked set for another nine championship points. But a punctured tyre five laps from the finish sent him into the pits, handing victory to Laffite's Ligier. Alan resumed to finish third behind team-mate Reutemann with Piquet fourth. The Brazilian was now seven points behind Jones in the title chase, and by no means out of the picture.

It all went right for Jabouille at the Österreichring, where he scored the marque's third win of the season with a beautifully judged performance. Conserving his

Discovery of the year was undoubtedly Alain Prost, although he was to quit McLaren at the end of the season, after a succession of worrying car breakages, and transfer to Renault.

141

THE HONOURS

machine with great self-discipline, he held off Jones by less than a second. Reutemann was third ahead of Laffite and Piquet. Alan emerged from the race some 13 points clear of the Brabham team leader. Qualifying in last place in his first grand prix at the wheel of a third Lotus entry was a tenacious young Englishman, Nigel Mansell. He struggled on doggedly, refusing to give up despite fuel leaking into the cockpit, only stopping when his engine failed.

Piquet was determined to give it his best shot and when Jones ran wide on the first lap of the Dutch Grand Prix at Zandvoort ripping apart his Williams's skirts he lost a lot of time in the pits. That effectively handed the race to Piquet. The Brazilian took the lead from Laffite's Ligier after a dozen laps and Arnoux pushed the Renault past into second place before the finish. Reutemann was fourth ahead of Jarier and Alain Prost in the one-off McLaren M30. Watson displayed a distinct upsurge of form, running mid-field before his engine expired after 18 laps, but Daly's Tyrrell had a massive accident at the end of the start/finish straight when one of his Tyrrell's brake calipers fell apart and deprived him of all stopping power. Shaken and bruised, he emerged otherwise intact.

Jones and Piquet neck-and-neck

Piquet was a mere two points behind Jones as they went into the Italian Grand Prix, on this occasion staged at Imola's Autodromo Dino Ferrari rather than its regular Monza venue. There was also enormous excitement among the passionately enthusiastic *tifosi* when the new Ferrari 126 turbo appeared during practice in the hands of Gilles Villeneuve. The chassis was rather rough and ready, but the engine clearly gave a great deal of power, pointing the way for the future.

Arnoux and Jabouille wrapped up the front row for Renault with Reutemann sharing the second rank with Giacomelli's Alfa Romeo, Bruno being joined by veteran compatriot Vittorio Brambilla for this home race. But Arnoux enjoyed a mere three laps in the lead before the confident Piquet sliced ahead and proceeded to out-run Jones and Reutemann by half a minute over the race distance. It was particularly worrying for Jones who now lost his points lead to the Brazilian with only two races left to run.

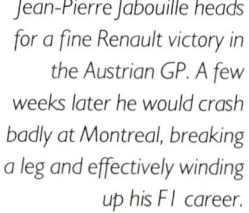

Jean-Pierre Jabouille heads for a fine Renault victory in the Austrian GP. A few weeks later he would crash badly at Montreal, breaking a leg and effectively winding up his F1 career.

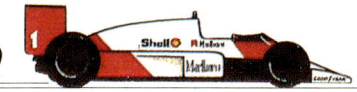

Completing the top six were de Angelis, Rosberg and Pironi, but Ferrari's outclassed 312T5s never had a chance. Villeneuve did his best for the first few laps before crashing heavily after a tyre exploded at 180mph. Briefly unconscious, he was very badly shaken by the episode. Likewise Scheckter, who had a similar massive accident in practice, but drove with enormous determination to finish an exhausted eighth, a performance even more impressive by the fact of his having already decided to retire from racing at the end of the season.

Tension ran high in Montreal where the two championship contenders qualified on the front row, Piquet ahead of Jones. Accelerating away from the line they touched going through the first S-bend causing Piquet to spear into the wall and triggering off a multiple accident which brought the race to a halt, obliging them to go through the psychological build-up all over again.

Jones's car was easily reparable, but Piquet had to take the spare Brabham fitted with a powerful, yet fragile, qualifying engine. It certainly seemed quick after the re-start, passing Jones after two laps and

pulling without any problem. Sure enough, the engine expired on lap 24, after which Alan's only challenge was making sure he got to the finish. Easing his pace, he allowed Pironi's Ligier to go ahead on the road, knowing that the Frenchman had been penalised for jumping the start. None the less, the chequered flag, and confirmation of a world championship won, certainly came as some relief.

Reutemann was second with Pironi classified third. Watson driving with rare brio, had forced his McLaren ahead of Carlos only to spin and drop to fourth. Villeneuve was an amazing fifth—having started 22nd on the grid—while sixth place fell to Mexican Hector Rebaque, who had taken over the second Brabham seat from Zunino in the middle of the season.

The following week Williams reinforced their world championship with a comfortable Jones-Reutemann 1-2 in the United States Grand Prix at Watkins Glen. Sadly, it was the last time the superb upstate New York track hosted a world championship single-seater race, which it had done every year since 1961.

Alan Jones celebrates his World Championship after victory in the Canadian GP. He is seen with Ligier's Didier Pironi, who finished ahead of him on the road, but was penalised back to third for an over-eager start.

143

THE HONOURS

1981

Continuing controversy over technical rules: Piquet takes first title: BMW builds turbo engine for Brabham

Elio de Angelis steers the controversial 'twin-chassis' Lotus 88 through the streets of Long Beach. The car never started a race, being deemed to contravene the technical regulations after a lengthy dispute.

Despite all the objections from British-based teams, FISA imposed new F1 technical regulations at the start of the 1981 season, which turned the year into a complex and expensive technical farce. It was naive of the sport's governing body to believe that the cars would somehow be safer without sliding skirts which, while being directly responsible for spectacularly high cornering speeds, at least made the cars progressive and manageable to control; but the new rule was imposed, together with a 6cm ground-clearance requirement.

Moreover, in an obvious attempt to tip the scales in favour of the heavier turbos, FISA raised the minimum weight limit to 585kg, an artificially high level for the non-turbo FOCA teams who had to ballast their cars to bring them up to regulation weight.

Of course, the additional weight and loss of sliding skirts should, theoretically at least, have handicapped the turbo brigade less. Their extra power would compensate for having to run extra large conventional aerofoils to sustain their aerodynamic downforce. The rule makers had reckoned without the ingenuity of the FOCA teams, however, in particular Brabham chief designer Gordon Murray, who designed a clever hydro-pneumatic lowering system, enabling Nelson Piquet and Hector Rebaque's Brabham BT49Cs to develop ground effect at speed, rising on their suspension before they came into the pit lane for a check on ground clearance.

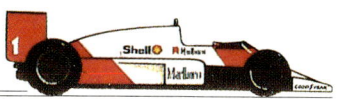

1981 DRIVERS' CHAMPIONSHIP

		points
1	Nelson Piquet	50
2	Carlos Reutemann	49
3	Alan Jones	46
4	Jacques Laffite	44
5	Alain Prost	43
6	John Watson	27
7	Gilles Villeneuve	25
8	Elio de Angelis	14
9	René Arnoux	11
	Hector Rebaque	10
11	Riccardo Patrese	10
	Eddie Cheever	10
13	Didier Pironi	9
14	Nigel Mansell	8
15	Bruno Giacomelli	7
16	Marc Surer	4
17	Mario Andretti	3
18	Patrick Tambay	1
	Andrea de Cesaris	1
	Slim Borgudd	1
	Eliseo Salazar	1

CONSTRUCTORS' CHAMPIONSHIP

		points
1	WILLIAMS	95
2	BRABHAM	61
3	RENAULT	54
4	LIGIER	44
5	FERRARI	34
6	McLAREN	28
7	LOTUS	22
8	ARROWS	10
	TYRRELL	10
	ALFA ROMEO	10
11	ENSIGN	5
12	THEODORE	1
	ATS	1

The Brabham team's opposition were up in arms about this lowering system, but FISA turned a blind eye to cockpit-operated jacking systems, thereby producing the ridiculous sight of stiffly-sprung ground effect chassis almost beating their drivers senseless over the bumps, only to be jacked up artificially to pass the ground-clearance test in the pit lane. Almost a decade later, the whole business seems even more incredible than it did at the time.

Before FISA and FOCA reached a compromise FOCA competed in the South African Grand Prix, run to the previous year's sliding skirt regulations. The event, won by Reutemann's Williams, was not counted for the world championship and no points were awarded which eventually made the difference between Carlos winning and losing the title.

The world championship proper got underway at Long Beach with the usual complement of new faces in fresh places. Andretti was partnering Giacomelli at Alfa Romeo, Mansell was on the full-time Lotus payroll and Prost had switched to Renault after a deal of legal wrangling with McLaren. Watson stayed with the British-based team which had amalgamated with Ron Dennis's Project 4 organisation to form McLaren International, with Andrea de Cesaris as number two driver. Eddie Cheever led the Tyrrell squad, and the Ferrari line-up was unchanged.

Riccardo Patrese surprised many people by putting his Arrows on pole position for the Californian race, but although he led in the early stages a blocked fuel filter put paid to his chances and Reutemann surged by for Williams. Carlos soon came under pressure from team-mate Jones, who nipped by to win after Reutemann made a slight mistake on a corner. Piquet was third for Brabham ahead of Andretti's Alfa, Cheever and Patrick Tambay's Théodore.

Reutemann had been annoyed at Jones muscling past him at Long Beach, so when he took the lead at the start of the rain-soaked Brazilian Grand Prix at Rio, he disregarded pit signals to let his team-mate through. He stayed ahead to the finish, breaching the terms of his contract and infuriating the Williams management, who imposed a hefty financial penalty when

Carlos Reutemann splashes past Chico Serra's abandoned Fittipaldi on his way to victory in the Brazilian GP – against team orders. Alan Jones was forced to follow him across the line on this occasion.

145

sharing out the prize purse.

Third place fell to Patrese ahead of Marc Surer, who did a fine job for the tiny, under-financed Ensign team. Piquet's Brabham started on pole position, but he incomprehensibly decided to start on slicks, gambling that the grey overcast would give way to dry conditions. He finished 12th, two laps behind Reutemann.

The move down to Buenos Aires for the Argentine Grand Prix was accompanied by endless controversy on two fronts. First, Colin Chapman's radical new 'twin chassis' Lotus 88, designed to get the best out of the new technical regulations, was finally outlawed by FISA after a three-race wrangle. Second, the new hydro-pneumatic suspension system on the Brabham worked a treat and Piquet breezed away to victory with ease. The system's advantage was graphically illustrated when Hector Rebaque, a grand prix journeyman, took the other Brabham BT49C through into second place ahead of Reutemann's Williams. Thankfully a broken distributor rotor arm prevented a travesty of a result, leaving Carlos to follow Piquet home second, claiming what Williams regarded as a moral victory. Many rival teams were outraged at what they saw as the Brabham suspension's illegality, but the result was allowed to stand and similar systems appeared on other machines by the time the championship battle resumed in Europe.

Nelson Piquet accelerates away ahead of Alan Jones's Williams at the start of the Argentine GP at Buenos Aires. The Brazilian won commandingly in a Brabham fitted with what many people regarded as illegal self-levelling suspension.

San Marino makes its bow

Encouraged by the response to their staging of the Italian Grand Prix the previous year, the Imola circuit authorities were authorised to run another race in 1981. With the Italian GP returning to its traditional home at Monza, the new event was titled the San Marino Grand Prix after the tiny mountain principality a short distance from the track. Team Lotus did not compete as Colin Chapman was re-trenching to construct new cars after the Type 88 had been banned. The British team owner's problems were compounded when his main sponsor was arrested for alleged financial impropriety. The partisan Italian crowd couldn't have cared less about Lotus's absence in this race, which marked the debut of future star Michele Alboreto at the wheel of a Tyrrell. Villeneuve delighted them by qualifying on pole position, leading the race in its rain-soaked early stages. Then Pironi took over at the front of the field before Piquet surged through to win. Villeneuve changed to slicks when it began to dry, only to have the rain start again, obliging him to make a second stop for wet rubber. But despite various problems Pironi wound up fifth behind Patrese and Reutemann, Villeneuve seventh. Jones trailed home 12th after deranging his nose wing against Reutemann

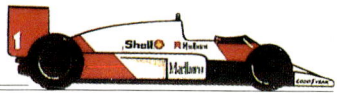

on the opening lap.

Reutemann was leading the points table, but his second win of the season at Zolder gave him little pleasure. During practice an Osella mechanic tripped and was hit and fatally injured by the Argentinian's Williams. It was not Reutemann's fault, but he felt the tragedy deeply. As if that wasn't enough, the Arrows team chief mechanic Dave Luckett, struggling to start Patrese's car, was run over on the starting grid by the second Arrows of Siegfried Stohr. Badly injured, Luckett survived to make a complete recovery.

Pironi led from the start, ahead of a close tussle between Piquet and Jones which ended with the Brabham sliding off the road after colliding with the world champion. Piquet was near-hysterical with fury, but Jones, who later crashed when the Williams jumped out of gear, shrugged aside his complaints. Thus Reutemann ran out the winner from Laffite's Ligier and Nigel Mansell, who scored the first championship points of his career after a fine performance. Reutemann now led the championship, 12 points ahead of Piquet, but it was a race he would have rather forgotten.

Piquet used a lightweight qualifying Brabham BT49C, disapproved of by the team's rivals, to grab pole from Villeneuve at Monaco, with Mansell's new Lotus 87 a splendid third. Unfortunately the Englishman was eliminated in an early bump with Reutemann's Williams and for much of the race the focus of attention was Jones's pursuit of Piquet's leading Brabham. Eventually the Brazilian slid into a barrier under pressure from the Williams driver. Alan admitted he laughed so much that he almost crashed himself, but Villeneuve eventually had the last laugh. Handicapped by a fuel system misfire, Jones lost the lead to the Ferrari, finishing second from Laffite and the lapped Pironi.

Villeneuve followed these heroic efforts with the unwieldy Ferrari 126CK by winning the Spanish Grand Prix at Jerez, taking the lead after Jones inexplicably spun away first place. With Laffite's pole-position Ligier JS17, Watson's fast rising new McLaren MP4, Reutemann and de Angelis's Lotus in tight formation in his wake, Gilles didn't put a wheel wrong to score a typically determined victory, a triumph of lightning reflexes over a poor-handling chassis.

Following the race Jean-Pierre Jabouille, still struggling to recover from the leg injuries he suffered when his Renault crashed at Montreal the previous year, announced his retirement. He had been over three seconds slower than Laffite in practice at Jarama and his place in the team was taken by Patrick Tambay.

The last win of Gilles Villeneuve's career came in the Spanish GP at Jarama. His Ferrari 126CK held back this train of cars, comprising Laffite's Ligier, Watson's McLaren, Reutemann's Williams and de Angelis's Lotus, for most of the race.

147

THE HONOURS

Prost and Watson advance

While the championship had developed into a Williams/Brabham battle, former McLaren team-mates Alain Prost and John Watson were busy enhancing their reputations. Prost had quickly eclipsed Arnoux at Renault, while the Ulsterman's lacklustre image had been rejuvenated with the arrival of the superb John Barnard-designed McLaren MP4. They both came into their own at Dijon-Prenois, the venue for the French Grand Prix, where Prost emerged the winner of a truncated, rain-interrupted race, chased home by the McLaren. Nelson Piquet was third ahead of Arnoux, and although Reutemann and Jones were out of the points, Carlos remained secure at the head of the points table.

At Silverstone the Lotus 88 controversy was propelled back into the limelight as Colin Chapman's slightly modified '88B' was re-presented for scrutineering and accepted for the British Grand Prix. Sadly, however, the RAC was immediately overruled by FISA and the cars had to be withdrawn and converted back to type 87 specification. Disappointingly, Mansell failed to qualify, but the home crowd had plenty to cheer about as Watson surged through to win when both Renault turbos faded. John had been fortunate not to be embroiled in a first-lap accident when Villeneuve's Ferrari spun and collected Jones's Williams, with de Cesaris also crashing the other McLaren

in trying to avoid the pile-up.

The BMW turbo-engined Brabham BT50 prototype was given its public debut in practice, but Piquet pursued his world championship hopes with the regular BT49C, crashing heavily while in third place behind the Renaults. In the end it was Reutemann who survived to finish second. The Argentinian was now 17 points clear, yet, incredibly, accepted a bet with the author against his own championship prospects. It was certainly a curious, yet rather revealing, gamble to take.

Of course, Jones could not be ruled out of the championship. After an early battle with Prost's Renault he went ahead at Hockenheim to dominate the German Grand Prix before his progress was blighted by yet another fuel system misfire. He gambled that a pit stop would cure the problem; it didn't, and he finished 11th.

Piquet notched up his third win of the season, moving closer to Reutemann, followed home by Prost, Laffite, Hector Rebaque and Eddie Cheever's new Tyrrell 011. However, at the Austrian Grand Prix Jacques Laffite became a world championship prospect with a timely win at the wheel of his Michelin-shod Ligier-Matra JS17. Both Renaults led, but Prost's front suspension broke, bringing him to a halt, fortunately without damage. Laffite pulled ahead of Arnoux to bag a crucial nine points, Piquet was third ahead of Jones and Reutemann, with the reigning champion grappling with a broken spring platform which made his Williams FW07C even more precarious to drive. Later

First of many: Alain Prost on the rostrum after his maiden F1 triumph in the French GP at Dijon-Prenois. On the right is John Watson, second for McLaren; on the left is Nelson Piquet, third for Brabham.

Jones condemned the rules which had bred such a generation of painful, rock-hard racing cars, hinting that he might retire, a decision to be confirmed the following month at Monza.

Prost bounced back into prominence with a fine victory at Zandvoort after an early battle with Jones for the lead of the Dutch Grand Prix. The Williams driver suffered tyre-wear problems which dropped him to third behind Piquet at the finish. Reutemann's and Laffite's title hopes receded when they collided as they disputed the line into the tricky Tarzan right-hander at the end of the start/finish straight; both were eliminated from the race.

A splendid run by Jones to second place at Monza behind Prost's more powerful Renault could not make up for Williams' disappointment at the Australians decision to retire at the end of the season. Alan drove brilliantly despite having had two fingers broken in a brawl the previous week, and when Piquet's engine expired on the last lap, Reutemann found himself promoted to third ahead of de Angelis. Reutemann, Piquet, Prost, Jones and Laffite were now covered by 15 points at the head of the championship table, with only two races left to run.

Michelin tyres usually performed better than Goodyears in the wet in 1981, so when the heavens opened before the start of the Canadian Grand Prix, Laffite rubbed his hands with gleeful anticipation. Jones burst into the lead at the start only to spin into retirement – and out of the championship – after a mere eight laps, handing the advantage to Prost's Renault. When Alain tangled with Mansell, Jacques's Ligier had a free run through to win from Watson and Villeneuve. The Canadian enjoyed a spectacular run during the course of which his Ferrari's nose wing progressively disintegrated and eventually flew off completely.

The championship shoot-out took place in the unlikely setting of a Las Vegas car park. The latest addition to the world championship fixture list was an improvised track in the car park of Caesar's Palace hotel/gambling complex. The torrid conditions made the race hard work for the contestants. When Reutemann destroyed the opposition with a blistering pole position lap, it seemed as though the moody Argentinian would have no problems clinching the title.

The grand prix was run to the accompaniment of media speculation that Jackie Stewart, James Hunt and Niki Lauda were all considering F1 comebacks. (In fact, once all the hubbub had died down, only Lauda, as expected, took up the F1 gauntlet and resumed his career.)

In the meantime Reutemann seemed to relinquish all his title aspirations once the Las Vegas race started. Jones led from start to finish while Carlos faded, inexplicably, to eighth place. Piquet, exhausted and dehydrated, struggled home fifth and took the world championship by a single point from the Williams driver.

Thus the season ended on a rather bewildering note. Piquet had driven well enough, unquestionably, but why Reutemann sat back and handed him the title remains a motor racing mystery.

Watson had several good races in 1981, apart from his Silverstone victory. His drive through the rain to second place behind Laffite in Canada was one of them.

1982

Niki Lauda returns: Andretti quits F1: Rosberg takes title with one win: FOCA boycotts San Marino Grand Prix

Welcome back! Niki Lauda on the rostrum at Long Beach with Keke Rosberg after beating the Williams driver into second place. It was only Niki's third race since his comeback after a two year lay-off.

After the intrigue and disagreement which had dominated the sport throughout 1981, most people in Formula 1 hoped that the political scene would be calmer in 1982. In fact it turned out to be an even more bitter and acrimonious year.

On the technical side the minimum-weight limit was reduced by 5kg to 580kg as a sop to the non-turbo FOCA-aligned teams, but even before the racing season began rumblings of discontent were heard, now

1982 DRIVERS' CHAMPIONSHIP

		points
1	Keke Rosberg	44
2	John Watson	39
	Didier Pironi	39
4	Alain Prost	34
5	Niki Lauda	30
6	René Arnoux	28
7	Patrick Tambay	25
	Michele Alboreto	25
9	Elio de Angelis	23
10	Riccardo Patrese	21
11	Nelson Piquet	20
12	Eddie Cheever	15
13	Derek Daly	8
14	Nigel Mansell	7
15	Carlos Reutemann	6
	Gilles Villeneuve	6
17	Andrea de Cesaris	5
	Jacques Laffite	5
19	Mario Andretti	4
20	Jean-Pierre Jarier	3
	Marc Surer	3
22	Manfred Winkelhock	2
	Eliseo Salazar	2
	Bruno Giacomelli	2
	Mauro Baldi	2
26	Chico Serra	1

CONSTRUCTORS' CHAMPIONSHIP

		points
1	FERRARI	74
2	McLAREN	69
3	RENAULT	62
4	WILLIAMS	58
5	BRABHAM	41
6	LOTUS	30
7	TYRRELL	25
8	LIGIER	20
9	ALFA ROMEO	7
10	ARROWS	5
11	ATS	4
12	OSELLA	3
13	FITTIPALDI	1

from some of the most prominent drivers.

Mario Andretti had quit the grand prix scene in favour of a total commitment to his first love, Indy cars, but it was a case of one out, one in as far as ex-world champions were concerned. As expected, Niki Lauda returned to the scene to partner Watson in the McLaren International line-up and it was the perceptive Austrian who drew the attention of Didier Pironi, president of the Grand Prix Drivers' Association, to a clause in the FISA licence form they were all supposed to fill in and sign. It seemed clear to Lauda, and subsequently to most of the drivers, that the conditions in these documents were far too

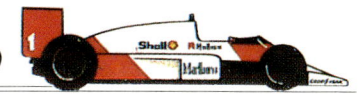

restrictive, and the net result was a boycott of the first day's practice for the South African Grand Prix at Kyalami. Eventually, faced in many cases with the prospect of being fired and/or sued for breach of contract by their team owners, the drivers went back to work.

Alain Prost's purposeful Renault RE30B made short work of the opposition, recovering from a pit stop to change a punctured tyre which dropped him back to eighth place. Carlos Reutemann's Williams FW07C, a logical evolution of the car which won its first race back in 1979, got through to second place ahead of Arnoux's Renault thanks to a mix-up in the French team's pit, and Lauda wound up a creditable fourth to launch his new career for McLaren. Keke Rosberg, signed by Williams to replace Alan Jones, finished fifth with Watson sixth. The new Ferrari 126C2s, designed by Englishman Harvey Postlethwaite, showed well in the early stages, but neither managed to finish and the BMW turbo-engined Brabhams proved similarly frail.

The 'water-bottle' affair

The next row brewed up at the Brazilian Grand Prix. To combat the more powerful turbos the front-running naturally-aspirated cars had adopted the technique of fitting water reservoirs, ostensibly for cooling

brakes. In fact, the water was used as ballast; early in the race it would be dispersed quickly in the general direction of the brakes, allowing the car to run beneath the minimum weight limit for the race. The reservoirs were topped up again before post-race scrutineering and the cars were apparently legal. Nelson Piquet, back in the Cosworth-engined Brabham BT49D for this race, and Keke Rosberg's Williams FW07C finished first and second at Rio only to find themselves disqualified, FISA eventually decreeing that such practices contravened the minimum weight regulations. The disqualifications gave Prost—who was third past the chequered flag—his second win of the year for Renault. Villeneuve's unwieldy Ferrari had led the first half of the race before succumbing to pressure from Piquet's featherweight Brabham.

Before FISA finally adjudicated on the 'water-bottle' affair, Niki Lauda reaffirmed his talent with a typically canny victory at Long Beach, beating Rosberg's Williams and Villeneuve's Ferrari, which was subsequently disqualified for a rear wing dimensional infringement. Andrea de Cesaris raised Alfa Romeo's hopes by starting from pole position, but the unpredictable Italian crashed after Lauda had taken over the lead from him. After the Brazilian race Reutemann abruptly decided to retire from motor racing, and his place at Long Beach was taken over by Mario Andretti before Irishman Derek Daly was signed to drive

The Renaults of René Arnoux and Alain Prost lead the Ferraris of Villeneuve and Pironi, and the rest of the field, on the first lap of the South African GP at Kyalami.

Controversial win: Didier Pironi snatches the lead in the San Marino GP from Gilles Villeneuve – against team orders. It caused considerable rancour between the two men and the rift was not healed before Gilles's death only a fortnight later.

alongside Rosberg for the rest of the season.

Prost now led the championship points table from Lauda, but the FOCA-aligned teams boycotted the San Marino Grand Prix at Imola in protest at FISA's decision over the brake-cooling controversy. The local crowd couldn't have cared less, being treated to a breathtaking three-way battle between Arnoux's Renault and Pironi's and Villeneuve's Ferraris. Eventually René joined team-mate Prost in retirement, leaving the Ferrari drivers to slog it out to the finish.

On the last lap a furious Villeneuve was pipped to the chequered flag by Pironi, against team orders in the Canadian driver's opinion. The post-race atmosphere was a curious blend of elation and indignation, rounding off a generally unsatisfactory weekend which was also highlighted by the sole FOCA team boss present, Ken Tyrrell (who'd broken ranks because of sponsorship considerations), submitting a protest against the legality of turbocharged engines as a whole.

This specious contention, concocted by FOCA's legal advisers as a tit-for-tat response to FISA's ruling about disposable ballast, rumbled away in the background for most of the summer. The anti-turbo lobby eventually determined to take its case to the International Chamber of Commerce in Lausanne, the final court of appeal under the Concorde Agreement, the recently forged 'F1 charter' which was supposed to put grand prix racing's house in order. Eventually FISA's viewpoint was quite predictably upheld and, within another couple of years, turbos were to become the only means of sustaining a team's competitiveness.

There was a tragic sequel to the Pironi/Villeneuve rift during final Belgian Grand

Prix practice at Zolder. Now treating like any other rival the team-mate who he believed had wronged him, Villeneuve collided with Jochen Mass's March as he battled to match Pironi's time. His Ferrari somersaulted to destruction over the slower car's rear wheel, fatally injuring Gilles. The Italian team naturally withdrew from the race, leaving John Watson's McLaren to score a well-judged win after Keke Rosberg's debutant Williams FW08 slid wide at a corner a couple of laps from the finish.

There were spins and incidents galore at Monaco, but thankfully nobody was injured and the outcome was in doubt right to the last lap. Prost looked as though he had it in the bag for Renault before unaccountably losing control and crashing heavily; Pironi and de Cesaris ran out of fuel, and Patrese's Brabham-Cosworth spun at the tight Loews hairpin; but Patrese managed to restart his machine and score his first win. Mansell, who would otherwise have won, was placed fourth behind Pironi and de Cesaris.

Watson's finest

The streets of America's motor city provided the next new venue for the roar of F1 exhausts when the world championship circus moved to Detroit for the first grand prix on the bumpy road circuit. It was something of a makeshift affair which endured on the international calendar for seven years, but few would pretend it was their favourite event. Alain Prost, in particular, developed a keen dislike of its claustrophobic atmosphere, although he planted his Renault firmly on pole position for the first race and led for six laps until Patrese and Roberto Guerrero's Ensign were involved in independent, minor accidents. The organisers over-reacted, showed the red flag and the race was stopped.

Prost led the re-start for many laps until slowed by a misfire, allowing Rosberg ahead, but on this day John Watson was not to be denied. Passing car after car, the Ulsterman drove the race of his life to win from Cheever's Ligier, Pironi's Ferrari and Rosberg, whose Williams was slowed with locking brakes and gear selection bothers. Lauda crashed when trying to keep up with his McLaren team-mate, whose victory propelled him to the top of the championship points table for the first time, six points clear of Pironi.

Incredibly, a host of minor technical problems prevented Nelson Piquet qualifying the

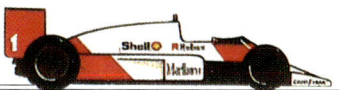

Brabham-BMW BT50 turbo at Detroit, the first time a reigning world champion had failed to make the cut since Scheckter at Monaco over two years earlier. But in a remarkable turnaround seven days later Piquet won the Canadian Grand Prix in faultless style, heading his Cosworth-Ford-engined team-mate Patrese across the line in gathering darkness for a Brabham 1-2. But it was another race that most people preferred to forget.

Pironi's Ferrari qualified on pole, but as the starting signal was given he stalled. Some lurid moments followed as other cars swerved round the stationary red car, but Italian novice Ricardo Paletti's Osella slammed straight into the back of it, erupting in flames. Out came the red flags yet again and track workers concentrated on dousing the conflagration. Paletti was flown to hospital, but sadly died of his injuries.

Remarkably, the stoic Pironi took over the spare Ferrari for the re-start, leading the first lap before Arnoux went by in the Renault. Piquet went into the lead on lap nine, however, and stayed there, the very cool conditions proving ideal for his new BMW turbo. Watson was third behind Patrese and, with Pironi fading to eighth, his points lead had swollen to 10. A minor casualty of

the day was Nigel Mansell, whose Lotus collided with Bruno Giacomelli. The Englishman's wrist was injured when his hand was caught in the steering wheel, forcing him to miss the French Grand Prix, where he was replaced by Geoff Lees.

The long straights and open sweeps at Zandvoort were clearly turbo territory and although Pironi qualified only fourth, he commanded the Dutch race in style to win from Piquet and Rosberg, with Lauda fourth. Watson, who had been the victim of an unpleasant hoax when a mischief-maker telephoned the BBC the night before the race to say he had been killed in a road accident, was out of the points on this occasion. The race ended with a heated pit lane discussion between Daly and Alboreto, who tangled on the last lap to finish fifth and seventh respectively. A second Ferrari was now on hand, Frenchman Patrick Tambay taking over Villeneuve's position to finish eighth on his maiden outing with the team.

Rosberg had by now really got the hang of the Williams FW08 and proved a sensation at Brands Hatch, qualifying on pole position for the British Grand Prix. Brabham, meanwhile, raised a few eyebrows when their BT50-BMWs arrived fully equipped for in-race refuelling: designer Gordon Murray

John Watson powers through the streets of Detroit during the first Grand Prix to be run in Motor City. He went on to complete the most commanding victory of his F1 career.

153

Top Patrick Tambay boosted Ferrari's sagging morale by winning the German GP at Hockenheim on the day after Pironi was badly injured in a practice shunt. Tambay is seen here in the Dutch GP.

Above Elio de Angelis just holds off Keke Rosberg to score Team Lotus's first win since 1978. It was the last of the team's triumphs to be witnessed by Lotus chief Colin Chapman, who died the following winter.

had calculated an overall gain in performance if they started with light fuel loads and stopped during the race for replenishment.

After Rosberg's Williams agonisingly refused to start before the parade lap, forcing him to start from the back of the grid, Piquet breezed off into an early lead. Both Brabhams retired early (Patrese in a startline shunt), however, so Murray's strategy was never put to the test. Niki Lauda wound up the winner from Pironi and Tambay's Ferraris, de Angelis's Lotus, Daly's Williams and Prost's Renault. The highlight of the day was Derek Warwick's performance in the Toleman-Hart TG181B: the Hampshire driver pulled through to second place behind Lauda before retiring – officially with a drive-shaft failure. Most people believed he was out of fuel after a morale-boosting half-tanks run on home ground, but there was certainly no question mark over his ability as a driver.

Watson spun out of the race early on, allowing Pironi to end the day at the head of the championship points table. The French-

man went to Paul Ricard and consolidated his advantage in the French Grand Prix, finishing third behind the Renaults of Arnoux and Prost.

This was another controversial event, which Arnoux won despite having agreed to follow Prost home to preserve Alain's increasingly slender title hopes. When Prost was slowed in the early stages with a damaged side skirt on his car, Arnoux raced ahead. Alain trusted him to slow up and concede, only realising he had been duped when it was too late. The atmosphere between the two men was very strained for the rest of the year. In a collision between Jochen Mass's March and Mauro Baldi's Arrows the March landed hard up against a spectator fence, mercifully causing only light injuries. But the speed and lack of controllability of the current breed of rock-hard F1 cars were highlighted yet again, as they had been after Villeneuve's fatal accident at Zolder. There was worse to come, however.

Leading the championship, Didier Pironi arrived at Hockenheim brimful of confidence for the German Grand Prix. Yet that dour, inhospitable circuit added him to its list of victims during rain-soaked practice when he struck the back of Prost's Renault at high speed, shattering both his legs as the Ferrari cartwheeled to destruction.

Renault frustration

It was another traumatic episode for the beleaguered Italian team which had not yet recovered from the shock of Villeneuve's loss. But Patrick Tambay administered a timely tonic the following day by winning the German Grand Prix, boosting morale at

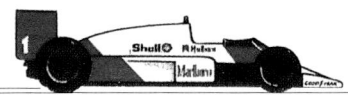

a crucially important moment. He won after Piquet's Brabham tripped over Chilean driver Eliseo Salazar's ATS at the Ostkurve chicane when lapping the slower car. Nelson erupted from the cockpit and physically assaulted his startled rival in an incident which was unfortunately televised world-wide.

The Austrian Grand Prix which followed was a happier event. Theoretically it should have been a turbo benefit, but on the superfast Österreichring the Brabhams, Renaults and Ferrari all hit troubles of varying degree. Prost's retirement from the lead five laps from the finish opened the door to a down-to-the-wire battle for glory. Scoring the first Lotus victory for four years, de Angelis held off Rosberg's Williams by one-twentieth of a second. But the Finn moved up into second place in the points table behind the injured Pironi, with Watson slumping to third after yet another retirement. Keke now looked favourite for the title—but had yet to win his first grand prix.

Renault, meanwhile, were getting increasingly desperate about their big-budget grand prix effort. Time and again either Arnoux or Prost led, yet seldom won. Prost almost won the Swiss Grand Prix (held at Dijon-Prenois in France as motor racing had been banned in Switzerland after the 1955 Le Mans disaster) with a little help from the man holding the chequered flag. Prost had handling problems as Rosberg gobbled up his lead in the closing stages, but the vigilant Williams team manager Peter Collins saw an official unfurling the chequered flag three laps from the finish. Suspecting that he might be about to flag the race to a premature finish—thus favouring the Renault—Collins hurried to restrain him. Rosberg passed Prost with two laps to go to win his first grand prix and take the title lead with 42 points. Prost had 41 with Lauda and Watson tying on 30.

Arnoux by now had dediced to leave Renault and join Tambay at Ferrari the following year, so his winning the Italian Grand Prix at Monza was regarded as something of a home success, even though he was driving a French car at the time. But, for the enthusiastic Ferrari fans, the real treat was the guest appearance of Mario Andretti at the wheel of the second Ferrari. The American, a regular Ferrari team member 11 years earlier, proved that at 42 he could still get the job done, qualifying on pole position and finishing third behind Tambay. The race also marked the debut, fleetingly, of the Alfa Romeo V8 turbo in practice and, more significantly, the announcement of a deal between McLaren and the Franco-Saudi high-technology group Techniques d'Avant Garde (TAG) to fund a Porsche-built F1 turbo engine. (Two years on it would take Formula 1 by storm.)

With nine points in hand over Watson, Rosberg went to Las Vegas for the final race of the year in a commanding position. To take the title John needed to win with Keke failing to score any points. It was too long a shot. Keke wound up fourth, clinching the championship with 44 points. Watson gave it everything, but was second in the race behind Michele Alboreto's Tyrrell. Yet, for all their problems, Ferrari had won the constructors' championship, with Rosberg's entrant, Williams, only placed fourth!

Michele Alboreto with Diana Ross on the rostrum after winning at Las Vegas. John Watson (right) was second, Eddie Cheever (left) third.

155

1983

Piquet wins first turbo title: Regulations require flat-bottomed F1 cars: Watson wins last Long Beach GP

Grand Prix racing moved into politically calmer waters at the start of 1983. The most significant technical change was the rule that all cars should have flat undersides to their monocoques, significantly reducing the ground effect developed by the wing-section side pods originally pioneered by Colin Chapman. Sadly, the Lotus boss was no longer on the scene to blaze new trails of technical innovation. Shortly before Christmas 1982 he had died of a sudden heart attack at the age of 54.

He left his team the legacy of a Renault turbo engine supply deal, but the famous Norfolk *équipe* had a troubled couple of years before the fruits of this development began to pay off.

The 1983 world championship battle was fought out between Brabham (retaining Piquet and Patrese), Renault (which signed Cheever to join Prost) and Ferrari (Arnoux and Tambay). Toleman also began to make their presence felt on an F1 scene where pit stops for fuel, pioneered by Brabham, soon became a complex part of an overall race strategy.

The new regulations posed designers the challenge of clawing back some of the lost downforce by more conventional aerodynamic means. The flat-bottom rules had been finalised relatively late and the Brabham team were the first to profit by them, four months of non-stop activity producing the striking new BT52 in time for the first race of the season in Brazil.

Although world champion Keke Rosberg managed to squeeze his revamped Williams

Keke Rosberg elected to run on slick tyres from the start of the Monaco GP, gambling that the damp track surface would dry. His audacity was rewarded with a remarkable victory in this naturally aspirated Williams FWO8C.

1983 DRIVERS' CHAMPIONSHIP

		points
1	Nelson Piquet	59
2	Alain Prost	57
3	René Arnoux	49
4	Patrick Tambay	40
5	Keke Rosberg	27
6	John Watson	22
	Eddie Cheever	22
8	Andrea de Cesaris	15
9	Riccardo Patrese	13
10	Niki Lauda	12
11	Jacques Laffite	11
12	Michele Alboreto	10
	Nigel Mansell	10
14	Derek Warwick	9
15	Marc Surer	4
16	Mauro Baldi	3
17	Danny Sullivan	2
	Elio de Angelis	2
19	Johnny Cecotto	1
	Bruno Giacomelli	1

CONSTRUCTORS' CHAMPIONSHIP

		points
1	FERRARI	89
2	RENAULT	79
3	BRABHAM	72
4	WILLIAMS	38
5	McLAREN	34
6	ALFA ROMEO	18
7	TYRRELL	12
	LOTUS	12
9	TOLEMAN	10
10	ARROWS	4
11	THEODORE	1

FW08C onto pole position and lead for the first few laps, he was quickly overtaken by Piquet, and when the Finn's car was briefly delayed by a fire by its fuel stop, Nelson was left to win easily in front of his home crowd. Keke followed him across the line only to be disqualified for a push-start, so Niki Lauda moved up to claim the official second place with Williams new-boy Jacques Laffite third from Tambay's Ferrari.

Tambay led the field at Long Beach before being savaged into retirement by the over-ambitious Rosberg, who had already spun 360 degrees without losing his second place on the opening lap. The net result of this curious event, where race tyre choices proved crucially important, was a Watson-Lauda McLaren 1-2 after the two drivers had sliced through the field from lowly 22nd and 23rd starting positions. Arnoux's Ferrari survived to finish third ahead of Laffite and Surer, leaving Lauda leading the championship after two rounds, a single point in front of Piquet. Alan Jones briefly returned from retirement to drive an Arrows in this event, but the team's subsequent failure to raise sponsorship for him prevented this from blossoming into a regular partnership.

The first European round of the championship took place at Paul Ricard in unseasonably cool weather for the south of France in April. Ferrari and Renault joined the fuel-stop brigade in time for this race. The technique helped Prost to lead commandingly throughout at the wheel of the impressive new Renault RE40, and the French team were prevented from scoring a 1-2 only by Piquet's Brabham beating Cheever back into third place. Tambay underlined the turbo brigade's strength by finishing fourth with Keke Rosberg, who, the previous weekend, had won the non-title Brands Hatch Race of Champions in which the first non-turbo home came fifth.

Despite this success, the Brabham BT52 was beginning to look the most consistently impressive car of the year and when Nelson Piquet stalled on the starting grid at Imola, it seemed as though Riccardo Patrese's golden moment had arrived. But the Italian's dreams of a home victory were brought to an abrupt end when, with leader Tambay's Ferrari in his sights, he slid off the road with a handful of laps to run. Prost's Renault came home second after Arnoux spun his Ferrari and Rosberg wound up fourth.

Keke was fighting an uphill battle against superior turbo power, but gambled superbly at the start of the Monaco Grand Prix. The Finn qualified sixth and from the start ran

Michele Alboreto's victory for Tyrrell (in Benetton livery) in the Detroit GP was the last non-turbo win until naturally aspirated engine regulations were re-introduced in 1989.

slick tyres on a still-soaking track surface when most of his major rivals were on deep-grooved rain tyres. The rain held off, the track dried out, and Keke, opposite-locking his way through the confined, barrier-lined streets with virtuoso precision, scored a memorable victory. Piquet wound up second from Prost and Tambay and American Danny Sullivan, running for Tyrrell alongside Alboreto, scored his first (and only) championship points with fifth place.

Prost profits at the new Spa

After an absence of 13 years the Belgian Grand Prix returned to the heavily revamped Spa-Francorchamps circuit for the next round of the title chase, the spectacular course in the Ardennes pine forests sustaining its reputation as no place for the unwary. Prost took pole position, but de Cesaris's Alfa Romeo V8 hurtled away into the lead from the start, only relinquishing his advantage at his routine fuel stop. Fuel-injection failure subsequently sidelined the Italian car, allowing Prost an unchallenged victory ahead of Tambay, Cheever and Piquet. Rosberg and Laffite rounded off the

points scorers with heroic fifth and sixth places in their naturally-aspirated Williams FW08Cs.

Cosworth came up with a new version of their 14-year-old V8 at Spa, the DFY, which was tried in Michele Alboreto's Tyrrell during practice. It had been developed in anticipation of FISA's avowed intention of restoring parity between the turbos and naturally-aspirated cars by 1985, but this was a forlorn hope. Michele Alboreto's rather lucky victory in the following Detroit Grand Prix was to be the last victory for a naturally-aspirated car until FISA finally outlawed turbos at the end of 1988.

The start at Detroit was something of a fiasco, with first de Cesaris's Alfa and then Tambay's Ferrari stalling on the grid. Piquet led from the start, planning a non-stop run in this race where fuel capacity was not a problem, but Arnoux—who planned to stop—quickly went through and built up a lead of almost half a minute before stopping for fuel and tyres. He resumed with his lead intact, only to retire shortly after with an electrical problem. Just as Piquet was congratulating himself on the Brabham strategy, a rear puncture forced him to make a stop anyway, and Alboreto, Rosberg and Watson winged past before he could get back out onto the circuit.

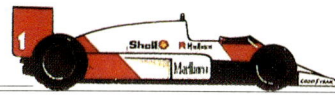

A proposed New York Grand Prix by now having fallen through, the F1 fraternity had its last outing of '83 in North America the following weekend. René Arnoux made up for his Detroit disappointment by leading the Canadian Grand Prix from start to finish, beating Cheever and Tambay into second and third places. With Prost a troubled fifth, Piquet could console himself that retirement with a broken throttle cable at least hadn't damaged his championship chances too badly. At the end of the North American tour Alain led by a scant three points, with Piquet and Tambay joint second.

The British Grand Prix at Silverstone was severely criticised for serving the paying public badly, a trend which was not unique to the English circuit. The paddock area was now impenetrably fenced off, bearing testimony to grand prix racing's increasing inclination to isolate itself from its public, with television coverage now the number one priority.

Honda engines return to Formula I

Arnoux and Tambay buttoned up the front row for Ferrari, but used smaller than usual rear wings for the race, which proved to be mistaken. Suffering from excessive tyre wear, they lost grip and dropped away, allowing Prost to win from Piquet. Tambay was third with Arnoux fifth, the two Italian machines split by Nigel Mansell's debutant Lotus 94T-Renault, a brand new car. Hur-

riedly conceived by the British team's new technical director Gérard Ducarouge to replace the original, unwieldy Renault-powered challenger, the Pirelli-shod 94T transformed Lotus's fortunes, helping Mansell and his team-mate de Angelis to demonstrate their true potential. The race also marked the return of Honda to the F1 championship: its V6 turbo powered the Spirit driven by Stefan Johansson. Within a few weeks Honda announced a long-term contract with the Williams team.

All was not well at Ferrari, however, where Enzo Ferrari had indicated his intention of signing Alboreto for 1984. The original

Top The Ferraris of Arnoux and Tambay lead away at the start of the British GP at Silverstone, but the race fell to Alain Prost's Renault RE40, seen *(above)* winning the Austrian GP, the French marque's last F1 success.

159

THE HONOURS

René Arnoux's Ferrari 126C3 on its way to victory in the Dutch GP at Zandvoort, the Frenchman's third win of the season, which helped retain his place in the Italian team for 1984.

plan was to drop Arnoux, but by the end of the year he had notched up three wins to Tambay's two, so even though Patrick had gained a reputation as a highly respected test and development driver, he was the one to be shown the door at Maranello.

Tambay had his first problem at Hockenheim where Arnoux won for a second time that season while he suffered engine problems. De Cesaris's Alfa took a surprising second place, followed by Patrese and Prost. Patrick then led the Austrian Grand Prix in masterly style before retiring again, this time letting Prost through to win from Arnoux, Piquet, Cheever and Mansell.

Prost still led the title chase with 51 points, 14 ahead of Piquet, but Alain was a worried man. Having seen Piquet's Brabham at the Österreichring he reported, shrewdly as things turned out, that if Renault wanted to win the championship they would have to do a lot more work to keep on top of BMW.

Of course, world championship titles are won by a crucial blend of driver and car: even if Renault's engine development was

lagging slightly, Prost also made a crucial driving error at the Dutch Grand Prix that compounded his concern. Attempting to overtake Piquet for the lead, he collided with the Brabham and bounced it into retirement, but in so doing damaged his Renault's nose wings and himself understeered into the guard rail less than a lap later. Arnoux won from Tambay, Watson and Derek Warwick, who scored his and Toleman's first-ever points. Prost was now eight points ahead of Arnoux, but feeling less confident after a race which had also marked the promising competition debut of the TAG/Porsche turbo powering an interim McLaren driven by Niki Lauda.

Piquet hits the front

Patrese qualified on pole at Monza, but Piquet wasn't to be denied in the race. He led throughout, chased home by Arnoux and Cheever, but Prost's Renault succumbed to engine failure and the Frenchman was feeling the pressure, escorted for

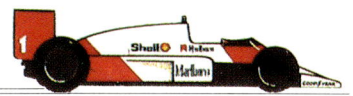

much of a rather tense weekend by armed bodyguards after death threats. With two rounds of the championship left Prost had 51 points, Arnoux 49 and Piquet 46.

Alain's worst fears were confirmed in the Grand Prix of Europe at Brands Hatch. Pole position was taken by de Angelis's promising Lotus 94T from Patrese, Mansell's Lotus and Piquet's Brabham. Prost could manage no better than eighth place and was only too aware that the Renault V6 was no longer a match for the highly-tuned BMW four-cylinder turbo powering the Brabham. There had been question marks over the legality of the special fuel used by BMW, (later laid to rest) and, come the race, Piquet sped to an unchallenged win after Patrese and de Angelis tripped over each other.

Prost finished second, but knew that only a miracle—or some atrocious luck for Piquet—could preseve his championship as the final race in South Africa loomed. Yet Renault's optimism proved almost embarrassing to Alain. An avalanche of French journalists were flown to Kyalami in the confident anticipation of a great French triumph and major national advertising campaigns were all set to go, trumpeting the imminent Renault success. They were riding for a spectacular fall.

Away from the spotlight of attention, Williams turned up in South Africa with their first Honda-engined challengers for Keke Rosberg and Jacques Laffite. The Finn qualified a promising sixth, only one place behind Prost, and Tambay's Ferrari took pole from Piquet, Patrese and Arnoux. Brabham boss Ecclestone had decided on a 'win or bust' strategy to destroy the opposition in the opening stages of the race. Piquet was to start on soft rubber with a minimal fuel load, run away in the opening stages, stop early for fuel and win the championship as a result. It worked like a dream: he stopped for fuel and tyres on lap 28 of the 77-lap race, by which time Prost, running fourth, was already in trouble. The Renault eventually limped into ignominious retirement with engine failure and, to make sure of his title, Piquet dropped back to finish a prudent third, allowing his team-mate Patrese the last win of the year with de Cesaris second. Niki Lauda's McLaren-TAG indicated what was in store for the future, climbing to second place before electrical problems sidelined him with six laps to go.

Renault foolishly made Prost the scapegoat for its failure to win the championship and he left the team within a week. He was snapped up by McLaren within hours in a move that proved to be the absolute making of his career. Many more race wins remained for the Frenchman—but not for Renault.

Nelson Piquet scored a first-time-out victory with the striking Gordon Murray-designed Brabham BT52 in Brazil – and went on to win his second World Championship with the car.

1984

		points
1	Niki Lauda	72
2	Alain Prost	71½
3	Elio de Angelis	34
4	Michele Alboreto	30½
5	Nelson Piquet	29
6	René Arnoux	27
7	Derek Warwick	23
8	Keke Rosberg	20½
9	Nigel Mansell	13
	Ayrton Senna	13
11	Patrick Tambay	11
12	Teo Fabi	9
13	Riccardo Patrese	8
14	Jacques Laffite	5
	Thierry Boutsen	5
16	Stefan Johansson	3
	Andrea de Cesaris	3
	Eddie Cheever	3
19	Piercarlo Ghinzani	2
	Jo Gartner	2
21	Marc Surer	1
	Gerhard Berger	1

CONSTRUCTORS' CHAMPIONSHIP

		points
1	McLAREN	143½
2	FERRARI	57½
3	LOTUS	47
4	BRABHAM	38
5	RENAULT	34
6	WILLIAMS	25½
7	TOLEMAN	16
8	ALFA ROMEO	11
9	ARROWS	6
10	OSELLA	4
11	LIGIER	3
12	ATS	1

Closest championship ever to Lauda: Fuel stops banned: Tyrrell disqualified from seasons's results: Senna arrives

For 1984, in an attempt to limit fast-mushrooming turbo power outputs, the maximum permissible fuel load was reduced from 250 to 225 litres and the potentially hazardous practice of refuelling during the race was outlawed.

McLaren's formidable team of young and old masters Prost and Lauda, now armed with the 'definitive' John Barnard-designed McLaren-TAG MP4/2s, faced some potentially strong opposition spearheaded by Piquet and Patrese in the Brabhams, Alboreto with Arnoux at Ferrari plus the all-new Renault line-up of Derek Warwick and Patrick Tambay.

Pre-season testing took place largely without the McLarens, for Barnard and Ron Dennis were playing their cards very close to their chests, and were reluctant to produce their new challenger until the last possible moment. It was thus one of the last contenders to arrive in Rio for the Brazilian Grand Prix and most of the media attention focused on Lotus and Ferrari, de Angelis and Alboreto making it an all-Italian front row ahead of Warwick's Renault, Prost, Mansell's Lotus-Renault and Lauda.

At the start Alboreto accelerated into an immediate lead which he held for 12 laps before spinning off when a front-brake caliper broke. Lauda's new McLaren then led until it retired with a minor electrical fault. Now Warwick went ahead, only for his Renault's front suspension to collapse, the possible legacy of an earlier bump with Lauda, just after Prost had gone past into a winning lead. It was left for Keke Rosberg's Williams-Honda FWO9 to finish second ahead of de Angelis and Cheever, now with Alfa Romeo. New boy Martin Brundle was fifth for Tyrrell on his first outing, but his

The McLaren-TAG MP4/2 was the dominant force throughout 1984, scoring 12 wins out of 16 races. Niki Lauda, seen here, took the drivers' title by half a point from team-mate Prost.

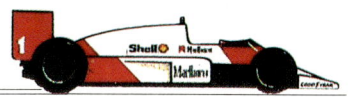

former F3 sparring partner Ayrton Senna retired his Toleman TG183B after only a handful of laps.

The brilliant young Brazilian, however, scored his first point with a sixth place at Kyalami, by which time the opposition was very worried about the speed, consistency and fuel-efficiency of the new McLaren-TAGs. It wasn't just that Lauda made up for his previous year's disappointment by winning the South African Grand Prix, but that Prost finished second. Alain had been forced to take the spare McLaren and start from the pit lane after his race car had given trouble on the warm-up lap. He breezed through the field to finish runner-up behind his team-mate, ahead of Derek Warwick's Renault and Riccardo Patrese's Alfa Romeo. The writing was very plainly on the wall, even at this early stage of the season.

Alboreto, who retired with fuel metering unit failure at Kyalami, successfully regained his Rio practice form for the Belgian Grand Prix, once more at Zolder. Qualifying his Ferrari 126C4 on pole ahead of team-mate Arnoux, the Italian led throughout to win from Warwick's Renault. Arnoux recoverd after a spin to finish third, ahead of Rosberg, who had made up time well after virtually stalling at the start.

McLaren dominance

Both McLarens retired with engine trouble on this occasion, but anybody who bet on that happening again with any regularity was going to lose money. The Brabham-BMWs, with their high-boost qualifying engines, were destined to be regular threats in qualifying, but the combination of the fine-handling McLaren chassis, the frugal TAG turbo engine and the expert assurance of Prost and Lauda in the cockpits proved simply devastating in the months that followed.

At Imola Prost won the San Marino Grand Prix despite taking time off for a 360-degree spin when problems with a faulty brake master cylinder briefly caught him out. Lauda was slow away from the start, but picked up the pace magnificently, moving up to fourth before his engine expired. At the finish Arnoux's Ferrari was the only other competitor on the same lap as Prost, with de Angelis third from Warwick. Ayrton Senna's Toleman failed to qualify after being caught out by the vagaries of a wet/dry practice session. In fact off-track controversy centred round Toleman's impending switch from

Pirelli to Michelin rubber, a change of allegiance which was completed in time for the French Grand Prix at Dijon, where their brand new TG184 chassis was scheduled to make its debut.

Renault put on a great show on their home ground: Tambay qualified on pole position and drove the race superbly, battling for the lead with Lauda and finally losing out to the McLaren only when he ran wide on one corner. Prost was delayed with an unscheduled pit stop after a heart-stopping moment when a front wheel worked loose, but he fought back to seventh. Nigel Mansell was third after a terrific performance, fighting grief over news of his mother's sudden death a few days earlier, while Arnoux could only earn fourth for Ferrari. Warwick crashed his Renault after a slight moment with Mansell, but emerged unscathed.

Those who imagine Monaco to be a sun-kissed millionaire's paradise on the verge of a shimmering Mediterranean were in for a nasty surprise when they turned up for the principality's grand prix: torrential rain fell throughout the race threatening to flood the track.

Most people were not surprised when the clerk of the course, Jacky Ickx, himself highly accomplished at racing in the rain, produced the chequered flag after half distance. Ayrton Senna probably didn't agree with him, though. The Brazilian rising star had his Toleman right up on Prost's tail, poised to overtake, when the event was halted. Mansell had been well placed, running faster than was necessary, when his Lotus skidded into a guard rail, while Stefan Bellof finished third for Tyrrell, making up for Brundle's failure to make the field after a massive qualifying accident.

A new star rises: Ayrton Senna on his way to sixth place in the Toleman TG183B in the South African GP – his second F1 race.

Mansell led the Monaco GP superbly for a while in his Lotus 95T, but he was trying too hard when he lost control on the climb to Casino Square and rattled the car along the barrier.

Lauda had spun off at Monaco and was now 10.5 points behind Prost, who had scored only half points (4.5) for his half-distance Monaco triumph. After the Monaco, there was a great deal of controversy about why the event hadn't been restarted in order to produce an aggregate result; but the Automobile Club de Monaco, already embroiled with FISA in a squabble over the race's television rights, deviated from the rule book and decided that the race was over. In what was generally regarded as an outrage within motor-racing circles, FISA later fined Ickx $6,000 and suspended his clerk of the course's licence for stopping the race without consulting the stewards.

North American interlude

Prost flew the Atlantic before the Canadian Grand Prix feeling in a strong position, but the McLarens were destined to be absent from the winner's spot on the rostrum at the next three races in Montreal, Detroit and Dallas, raising the hopes of the opposition. Nelson Piquet, his new Brabham BT53 handicapped by depressingly poor reliability from his BMW engine, managed to win the first two of those races, but Keke Rosberg's Williams-Honda emerged a surprise winner at Dallas on a circuit whose surface was crumbling like a meringue under the blistering Texas sun.

In Montreal Piquet beat Lauda and Prost into second and third places, and in Detroit won in a spare Brabham after a multiple start-line shunt, triggered by Mansell, propelled Nelson very heavily into a concrete barrier. Martin Brundle's Tyrrell rocketed

through to second place in this race, raising the young English driver's standing considerably; but there was only disappointment lying in wait for him and the team.

In Dallas Brundle crashed in practice, injuring both feet, but then Tyrrell became embroiled in a controversial dispute with FISA. After analysing the water tank contents of Brundle's Tyrrell after that second-place finish at Detroit, FISA decided that Tyrrell had been using illegal additives in what was thought to be a water-injection system spraying into the engine's intake trumpets. It had become the practice for Ken Tyrrell to run under the minimum weight limit in the early stages of the race to gain his naturally-aspirated cars a performance increment, the car then making a pit stop later in the race when lead shot was forced in under water pressure to ballast the car up once more.

It was an ugly episode which ended with Tyrrell having his world championship points score disallowed and being disqualified from the last three races of the season. Fading into historical perspective, it is widely regarded as a classic example of FISA's bull in a china shop approach to policing grand prix racing. Happily, it would take more than a skirmish with the sport's governing body to put down Ken Tyrrell and he bounced back, as expected, the following year.

The Dallas race was also memorable for Nigel Mansell's first pole-position start, the Englishman leading in fine style from the off. However, on the rostrum winner Rosberg made some uncharitable observations about what he considered Nigel's obstructive driving tactics. By that time Mansell was being tended at the medical centre for heat exhaustion, having collapsed attempting to push his out-of-fuel Lotus across the finishing line to claim an eventual sixth place. Later FISA fined Mansell $6,000 for causing the Detroit start-line shunt.

Apart from Rosberg's victory, the sole race to be held at Dallas will long be recalled for the punishment it meted out to many competitors. Lauda, Prost, Warwick, Tambay and Alboreto were among the many who fell victim to its unyielding concrete walls. Arnoux finished a brave second, but the Ferraris were badly out of luck on their return from North America for the British Grand Prix at Brands Hatch.

At this event a capacity crowd saw Piquet's pole position Brabham locked in a battle for the lead with the two McLaren-TAGs. The race had to be re-started after ten laps when novice Jonathan Palmer's RAM crashed heavily at Clearways. Prost's gearbox wilted, leaving Lauda to cruise home to an immensely popular second Brands Hatch victory for McLaren. Warwick's Renault wound up second ahead of Ayrton Senna,

Martin Brundle thought he had finished second at Detroit, but then found himself disqualified in an esoteric dispute concerning fuel additives. Later, at Dallas, he broke his ankles in practice and was out for the rest of the year.

Keke Rosberg, Grand Prix racing's great improviser of the 1980s, ran the gauntlet of a crumbling track surface to win the one-off Dallas GP in his Williams-Honda.

who displayed truly impressive form at the wheel of the Toleman TG184. The Ferraris of Alboreto and Arnoux finished fifth and sixth behind de Angelis's Lotus, having spent far too long boxed in behind the obstructive de Cesaris, now driving for the French Ligier squad.

Lauda and Prost head-to-head

The two-way battle for the championship really began to hot up at Hockenheim where Prost this time had the upper hand, beating his more experienced team-mate into second place. But on Lauda's home ground at the Österreichring Alain spun off on oil dropped by de Angelis's Lotus and Niki won, despite dire gearbox problems. Piquet, who eased off to finish second, was successfully duped into believing that Lauda was cruising to victory and, in consequence, failed to pick up the pace. Alboreto was third for Ferrari ahead of Teo Fabi's Brabham and the Arrows-BMWs of Thierry Boutsen and Marc Surer.

Lauda came away from Österreichring leading the championship points table at last, but the pendulum swung in Prost's favour at Zandvoort where Niki gambled on an incorrect tyre choice and was ten seconds behind the Frenchman at the chequered flag. Mansell and de Angelis finished third and fourth for Lotus. The weekend's big off-track story was that Ayrton Senna would be leaving Toleman at the end of the year to join Team Lotus. Mansell, in turn, would be moving to Williams to replace Laffite, the Frenchman returning to Ligier. Although there was a 'buy-out' clause in Senna's Toleman contract, the way in which he conducted his split with the team infuriated Toleman's management to the point where they suspended him from the Italian Grand Prix. Stefan Johansson, however, kept Toleman's end up superbly at Monza to finish fourth in a race which Lauda won yet again as Prost's engine expired. Niki drove a shrewdly calculating race, letting Piquet and Tambay set the pace in the early stages, only moving ahead when the Renault's throttle cable broke with eight laps to go. Sixth place was taken by Austrian new boy Gerhard Berger, guesting at the wheel of an ATS. Much more would be heard of this youngster!

The penultimate round of the championship battle was at the new Nürburgring, a bland and featureless autodrome whose construction necessitated bulldozing the whole start/finish area of the classic Nürburgring. The antiseptic new circuit found

few fans among the diehards, who thought it even less inspiring than Hockenheim.

Senna returned to the F1 fold for this race only to become embroiled in a massive first-corner shunt which also eliminated Rosberg's Williams, de Cesaris's Ligier and Berger. Prost led throughout from second place on the grid. Lauda qualified badly and spent much of the race battling through to fourth place, handicapped by losing time with a spin as he came up to lap Mauro Baldi's Spirit. After the race Niki took the matter up with the Italian driver, only to be non-plussed when Baldi stood his ground and told his more exalted rival that the episode had been entirely his own fault and he had nobody to blame but himself!

Lauda could have clinched the championship beyond doubt with a second place at the Nürburgring, but now Prost took the battle all the way to Portugal where a world championship grand prix was being staged for the first time since 1960. The venue was the Estoril autodrome, a few miles inland from the fashionable seaside resort of Cascais, and the grid was swollen by a third Renault entry for French F2 star Phillipe Streiff.

Piquet took pole position from Prost, Senna and Rosberg with Lauda well back yet again in 11th place. At the start Rosberg briefly took his bucking bronco of a Williams-Honda ahead, lurching precariously over the many bumps which abound on this challenging track, but the smooth Prost soon asserted himself at the head of the field.

Lauda, meanwhile, was finding that fiddling with his McLaren's cockpit turbo boost control made no difference to the engine's performance, which he found highly frustrating as he attempted to haul his way into contention through the mid-field runners.

By lap 33 of the 70-lap race Lauda was third with only Nigel Mansell's Lotus 94T separating him from Prost. On lap 52 the Englishman spun off with brake problems, so now all Niki had to do was to concentrate on finishing second. Prost, heading for his seventh win of the season, could do nothing more. At the end of the race the two McLarens cruised past the chequered flag 13 seconds apart, and Prost had to resign himself to missing the world championship by the wafer-thin margin of half a point.

In their quest for the constructors' title McLaren had established a record points' score, and between them Prost and Lauda had won 12 of the season's 15 races. As Niki's wife Marlene, making her first visit to a motor race for six years, congratulated the new champion, Ayrton Senna joined them on the rostrum, having taken third place on his final outing for Toleman. It was an achievement of considerable magnitude, underlining his long-term promise. Alboreto and de Angelis finished fourth and fifth, the Lotus driver winding up third in the title battle after a splendidly consistent season handled in a most mature manner. But, at the end of the day, the McLaren-TAGs had proved to be in a class of their own: and only Prost and Lauda had them.

Victory celebrations after Niki Lauda clinched his third World Championship at Estoril, 1984. Alain Prost (only half a point behind) and McLaren boss Ron Dennis share this golden moment.

167

1985

Prost wins title at last: First victories for Senna, Mansell: Honda consolidates partnership with Williams

Nigel Mansell prepares for his first race in a Williams, the Brazilian GP. It was the start of an exciting three-year partnership which netted 13 Grand Prix wins.

One of the most important aspects of the 1985 grand prix season was Michelin's withdrawal from Formula 1, leaving Goodyear to expand its supply arrangements to include McLaren and Renault. Toleman, who had built a brand new car to be driven

by Stefan Johansson, now faced a major dilemma. Having switched somewhat abruptly from Pirelli to Michelin, they now had to go cap in hand to their former suppliers as Goodyear did not have the capacity to supply them. Only when the team was sold to Italian-owned Benetton did Pirelli agree to restore its tyre supply contract.

Technical regulations were substantially unchanged, although fuel capacity was trimmed by another 5 litres to 220 litres maximum. Bernie Ecclestone's Brabhams were now running on Pirelli rubber, the product of a multi-million dollar deal by the shrewd Brabham team owner. Renault team manager Gérard Larrousse and engineer Michel Tetu had left Renault to join Ligier, leaving the French national F1 team struggling with its new RE50 chassis, while Tyrrell was back on the scene with a deal for Renault turbo-engine supplies later in the season. Gerhard Berger was now a full-time member of the F1 club, partnering Belgian Thierry Boutsen in the Arrows line-up.

At Rio Alboreto opened his championship challenge by planting the new Ferrari 156/85 on pole position, but it was Keke Rosberg in the new carbon-fibre Williams FW10 who powered into the lead at the start, only to retire after 10 laps with turbo failure. Mansell's career at Williams, meanwhile, had got off to a bad start, when he spun off after colliding with Alboreto on the run to the first corner, resuming only briefly before retiring. Alboreto and Prost were left to scrap for the lead, with the Frenchman coming out on top for the second year running. But Michele returned to Europe moderately confident that the latest Ferrari would give the McLaren-TAGs a run for their money.

Senna's first win

Torrential rain fell throughout the Portuguese Grand Prix at Estoril, this year the second round of the championship battle. Ayrton Senna qualified his Lotus 97T-Renault on pole position and led throughout in such dire conditions that even Prost pirouetted off when he acquaplaned on a huge puddle in the middle of the start/finish straight. Eventually Alboreto splashed through the murk to take second place behind the brilliant Brazilian with Patrick Tambay's Renault third ahead of Elio de Angelis in the other Lotus. Alboreto now led the title battle by three points from Prost and Senna. Jonathan Palmer made his debut for

1985 DRIVERS' CHAMPIONSHIP

		points
1	Alain Prost	73
2	Michele Alboreto	53
3	Keke Rosberg	40
4	Ayrton Senna	38
5	Elio de Angelis	33
6	Nigel Mansell	31
7	Stefan Johansson	26
8	Nelson Piquet	21
9	Jacques Laffite	16
10	Niki Lauda	14
11	Patrick Tambay	11
	Thierry Boutsen	11
13	Marc Surer	5
	Derek Warwick	5
15	Stefan Bellof	4
	Philippe Streiff	4
17	René Arnoux	3
	Andrea de Cesaris	3
	Ivan Capelli	3
	Gerhard Berger	3

CONSTRUCTORS' CHAMPIONSHIP

		points
1	McLAREN	90
2	FERRARI	82
3	WILLIAMS	71
	LOTUS	71
5	BRABHAM	26
6	LIGIER	23
7	RENAULT	16
8	ARROWS	14
9	TYRRELL	7

Marino Grand Prix. The Lotus and McLaren battled long and hard for the lead, Ayrton getting the upper hand only to run out of fuel with three laps to go. But there was an equally bitter flip-side to Prost's apparent triumph. His McLaren was found to be under the permitted minimum weight limit at post-race scrutineering and consequently disqualified, handing victory to Elio de Angelis in the other Lotus 97T. Thierry Boutsen just trickled past the chequered flag, his Arrows' fuel tank dry, to take second place with Tambay third ahead of a troubled Niki Lauda.

Senna started on pole position at Monaco, although he infuriated several of his more experienced rivals by cruising round to 'protect' his place at the front of the grid after setting the fastest time. Lauda and Alboreto were among those who expressed their anger at the young Brazilian's behaviour, but at the start of the race he took an immediate lead pursued by Michele's Ferrari and Prost's McLaren. However, Senna's engine, over-revved inadvertently during the race-morning warm-up, expired, leaving Alboreto and Prost to battle energetically for victory. Michele and the Ferrari were the faster combination but were delayed by a puncture and eventually finished second behind the McLaren. The consistent de Angelis was third, ahead of de Cesaris's Ligier and Warwick's Arrows. Piquet's Brabham and Patrese's Alfa Romeo collided spectacularly on the start/finish straight while battling for minor placings, both drivers emerging unscathed from the ensuing spectacular accident. This race also marked the return of Toleman, Teo Fabi giving the new TG185 its race debut.

What followed at Spa was without precedent in international motor-sport. After truncated practice sessions on the recently resurfaced track, which was crumbling under the strain of F1 activity, the stewards

the German Zakspeed team at this race, but retired early, while Stefan Johansson— released from his Toleman contract—replaced the temperamental René Arnoux in Ferrari's line-up after only one race of the season.

There was a nasty shock awaiting both Senna and Prost at Imola during the San

Ayrton Senna won two Grands Prix for Lotus in 1985, but was out of luck here at Montreal, where he was delayed by a pit stop to secure a loose turbo clip and finished out of the points.

THE HONOURS

postponed the Belgian Grand Prix, due to be held on 1 June. It was eventually run in the middle of September. In the sole official qualifying session before the meeting was abandoned Alboreto had set the fastest time at the wheel of his Ferrari.

In the Canadian Grand Prix at Montreal Alboreto and Johansson proved that the Ferraris were both fuel-efficient and fast, steaming home to score an impressive 1-2 triumph ahead of Alain Prost's McLaren. Keke Rosberg finished fourth after an early delay in an impressively more competitive Williams-Honda, which sustained its form to win the following weekend's race through the streets of Detroit. Frenchman Philippe Alliot was probably the luckiest man taking part in the Canadian Grand Prix, crashing his RAM heavily when exiting the fast S-bend beyond the pits but emerging unscathed.

Street-cred Keke

Senna took pole position for the Detroit race, an event in which he later scored a hat-trick of victories. But on this occasion, although he briefly held the lead in the opening stages, his race ended resoundingly and

painfully against a tyre barrier when he fell foul of the deteriorating track surface. Rosberg was always at his best in conditions needing versatile improvisation of driving technique and, in a performance which recalled his Dallas success the previous summer, juggled his Williams past the chequered flag ahead of Johansson's fast-closing Ferrari. Alboreto could manage only third place, but returned to Europe with 31 points in the title battle, seven ahead of de Angelis and nine in front of Prost.

By this stage in the season Nelson Piquet had found the Brabham team's switch to Pirelli a less-than-productive move: the tyres' performance seemed worryingly inconsistent from circuit to circuit. But they proved ideal at Paul Ricard under a sweltering French summer sun, and although Rosberg took pole position, over a second faster than the Brabham BT54, Nelson quickly pulled to the head of the pack once the race had started and kept there to the finish. Rosberg slammed by Prost's McLaren to take second place on the very last lap, a good result for Williams after near-tragedy during practice, when Mansell crashed heavily following a tyre failure at around 200 mph on the long back straight. The Englishman had been badly shaken and did

Keke Rosberg battles his way to victory at Detroit with the Williams-Honda FW10, yet another success in the mould of his 1984 Dallas victory.

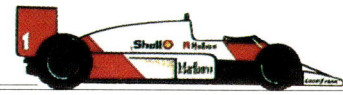

not take part in the race, although he recovered sufficiently to compete in the British Grand Prix at Silverstone a couple of weeks later. Johansson grabbed fourth place from de Angelis on the last lap, while Senna crashed spectacularly, his Lotus spinning on its own oil when the engine failed. The accident occurred at the same point on the circuit as Mansell went off, so the Brazilian was extremely fortunate to walk away. This race was also the debut of the Tyrrell-Renault driven by Martin Brundle.

Around the time of the British Grand Prix, FISA's concern over the ever-increasing F1 lap speeds prompted them to suggest bringing forward by a year the changes to the F1 technical regulations originally scheduled for the start of 1987. These involved the use of boost-control valves (known popularly as 'pop-off' valves) as well as smaller turbos and a 1,200cc capacity limit. Ferrari countered by threatening a switch to the U.S.-based Indy car series, and the threat of precipitate FISA action subsided, although when Keke Rosberg bettered an average speed of 160 mph in taking pole position for the Silverstone race, it was understandable that some people were highly concerned about F1 car performance.

In the race itself Senna powered into the lead from the start and the Williams-Hondas faded early on, leaving Prost to chase the Brazilian's Lotus. Ayrton later rated this as one of the most satisfying races of his career, even though it ended in disappointment when the Renault engine's electronic-management system went haywire and he ran out of fuel with six laps to go. Prost won easily, but Alboreto took a distant second to hang onto his lead in the points table; Laffite's Ligier was third from Piquet's Brabham.

In a return to the new Nürburging, Alboreto performed splendidly, his Ferrari recapturing its Monaco form to beat Prost in a straight fight to win the German Grand Prix. On the first corner he unfortunately nudged team-mate Johansson, sending the disappointed Swede heading for the pits to replace a deflated tyre, but otherwise he drove with an impressive blend of verve and confidence. Laffite, Boutsen, Lauda and Mansell completed the top six points scorers, while Alboreto looked more like a world-championship contender than ever before. Teo Fabi started the race from a surprise pole position in the Toleman-Hart, but never featured once the race got under way, while a third Renault entry, in the hands of François Hesnault, was allowed to take part

to test an on-board TV camera.

Before the Austrian Grand Prix RAM team leader Manfred Winkelhock died of injuries from a crash in his Porsche 962C during an endurance race at Canada's Mosport Park circuit. His place in the F1 line-up at the Österreichring was taken by Kenny Acheson. Off-track announcements included Niki Lauda's decision to retire—this time for good—at the end of the season, his place at McLaren to be taken by Keke Rosberg. Alerted by this news Frank Williams quickly signed up Nelson Piquet to replace the Finn

Below *Thanks to ideal Pirelli rubber and some long-overdue mechanical reliability, Nelson Piquet won the French GP in commanding fashion in this Brabham BT54.*

Bottom *Michele Alboreto (Ferrari 156/85) heads towards a memorable victory in the German GP, where he beat Alain Prost in a straight fight around the sanitised new Nürburgring.*

as lead driver for 1986; Nigel Mansell had already been contracted to stay for a second year, nominally as number two.

This year Lauda's luck failed in front of his home crowd. Prost just pipped Mansell's Williams-Honda to take pole position and the Frenchman grabbed an immediate lead. Although Lauda caught and briefly passed the other McLaren, the Austrian's TAG V6 suffered turbo failure, leaving the way clear for Ayrton Senna's Lotus 97T to finish second ahead of Ferrari twins Alboreto and Johansson. It was a crucial turning point in the title race, Prost now tying with Alboreto at the head of the championship points table, but with the Italian's mount looking less convincing with every race.

McLaren to the fore again

There had been indications during the summer of 1985 that Lauda was beginning to lose his competitive edge, but while that might have been true for the frantic, on-the-edge business of qualifying, the Dutch Grand Prix plainly emphasised that he liked winning races as much as the next man. The two McLarens were very much in charge of this particular event and when a sticking wheel nut allowed Niki to take the lead while Prost was delayed in the pit lane, the scene was set for an epic confrontation.

In the closing stages Prost pulled right up onto Lauda's tail, but there was no easy way past. The two experienced F1 hands went at it hammer and tongs like a couple of Formula Ford novices, Lauda emerging victorious by a matter of feet. Both men emerged from the cockpits of their cars beaming from ear to ear, Prost in the realisation that, second place or not, he had wrested the championship points lead from Alboreto's grasp.

Senna survived to finish third, despite an unfriendly nudge from Alboreto's Ferrari on the last lap; de Angelis was fourth and Mansell fifth. By now it was clear that the Williams-Hondas were capable of matching the McLaren-TAGs on most circuits, the Anglo-Japanese machines only needing an injection of mechanical reliability to make them potential world championship winners.

Fortunately for Prost it was too late for an upsurge in Williams-Honda form to affect the outcome of the title battle, but Alain certainly had his hands full at Monza during the Italian Grand Prix, where Rosberg proved the pace-setter and handed the McLaren driver another victory only after his engine failed less than 10 laps from the finish. Brabham, too, had a good day at Monza with Piquet and Marc Surer taking second and

Great moment for two on the rostrum after the GP of Europe at Brands Hatch: Nigel Mansell (left) has just won his first Grand Prix; Alain Prost (centre) his first World Championship.

fourth places, sandwiching Ayrton Senna's Lotus, while Johansson's Ferrari was fifth. Alboreto succumbed to engine failure, his championship prospects by now virtually snuffed out.

The Belgian Grand Prix was re-run in precariously wet conditions, giving Senna another opportunity to display his lightning reflexes on a slippery track. Prost took his first pole position of the year, a reflection of the McLaren's excellent chassis: the Porsche's development programme for the TAG turbo V6 set little store by qualifying performance, preferring to concentrate—with great success—on race performance.

Prost finished third behind Senna and Mansell, the Englishman scoring the best result of his career with the Williams-Honda despite aggravating the minor chest injury he had suffered at Monza when the FW10's steering wheel broke and he had a nasty moment wrestling it back under control. Sadly the race took place without Stefan Bellof, who had been killed when his Porsche crashed in the classic Spa 1,000km sportscar race a few weeks earlier.

Mansell's fast-rising prowess with the powerful Williams-Honda bore fruit at last when he won the Grand Prix of Europe at Brands Hatch, cheered on by thousands of his ecstatic fans. Senna was second, Rosberg an heroic third after a tangle with Piquet and Prost fourth, thereby becoming the first-ever Frenchman to win the world championship.

He achieved that distinction just in the nick of time. Seemingly transformed by his first GP success, Mansell started from pole position at Kyalami to win the South African race as well, and although a transmission breakage on the first lap forced Nigel out of the inaugural Australian Grand Prix at Adelaide, Rosberg was on hand to make it three in a row for Williams-Honda.

The Australian race proved a hugely popular addition to the world championship schedule, producing some worthwhile pointers to future form. Lauda almost won the final grand prix of his illustrious career, grabbing brakes causing the triple champion's McLaren to glance the wall when well ahead, so Keke took the win, with the Ligiers of Jacques Laffite and Philippe Streiff finishing second and third despite colliding on the last lap. Fourth, on his second GP outing for Tyrrell, was a bespectacled young Italian by the name of Ivan Capelli. Another star of the future had scored the first championship points of his career.

Keke Rosberg signed off from Williams by winning the inaugural Australian GP through the streets of Adelaide. Here he leads Nelson Piquet's Brabham and the badly out-of-shape Tyrrell-Renault of Martin Brundle.

THE HONOURS

1986

Prost wins second successive title: Mansell wins his spurs: Nine poles for Senna: Fuel allowance cut again

Speed with frugality was the key to Formula 1 success in 1986 when FISA once again slashed maximum permissible fuel capacity, this time from 220 to 195 litres. The engine builders, led commandingly by Honda, responded with enormous advances in the technology of their engine-management systems, sustaining phenomenal power outputs within the latest fuel-consumption constraints. Williams-Honda started the year as strong favourites, but, sadly, the team's boss was not on hand to see Nelson Piquet give the new FW11 a maiden victory in the Brazilian Grand Prix at Jacarepaguá.

Returning to Nice airport after the final pre-season test session at Paul Ricard, Frank Williams was gravely injured in a road accident. His life was feared for, but he now applied to the challenge of physical survival the enormous will and determination with which he had built his company from nothing into one of the most formidable racing teams in the world. Frank pulled through, but he was severly paralysed and confined to a wheelchair. Many months passed before he appeared again at the pit wall.

Piquet's victory at Rio was doubly satisfying for the Brazilian, yet in a sense it highlighted some problems which were to erupt with more serious implications in the months that followed. Firstly, his Williams-Honda easily beat Ayrton Senna's Lotus 98T-Renault into second place, but he also gained some wry amusement in watching team-mate Mansell spearing into a barrier mid-way round the second lap after fumbling an overtaking manoeuvre on Senna. Piquet seemed to have persuaded himself that the 1986 world championship would be a piece of cake. But, if that was the case, he had very seriously underestimated the strength of his opposition.

Third and fourth at Rio were the promising Ligier-Renaults of Jacques Laffite and René Arnoux, while Martin Brundle scored the first (official) points of his F1 career with fifth place for Tyrrell. Completing the list of points scorers was Gerhard Berger, now behind the wheel of a new Benetton-BMW.

Ayrton Senna beats Nigel Mansell to the line to win the Spanish GP at Jerez by the official margin of one-hundredth of a second.

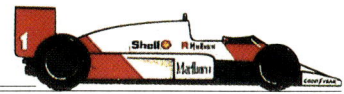

1986 DRIVERS' CHAMPIONSHIP

		points
1	Alain Prost	72
2	Nigel Mansell	70
3	Nelson Piquet	69
4	Ayrton Senna	55
5	Stefan Johansson	23
6	Keke Rosberg	22
7	Gerhard Berger	17
8	Jacques Laffite	14
	Rene Arnoux	14
	Michele Alboreto	14
11	Martin Brundle	8
12	Alan Jones	4
13	Johnny Dumfries	3
	Philippe Streiff	3
15	Teo Fabi	2
	Riccardo Patrese	2
	Patrick Tambay	2
18	Christian Danner	1
	Philippe Alliot	1

CONSTRUCTORS' CHAMPIONSHIP

		points
1	WILLIAMS	141
2	McLAREN	96
3	LOTUS	58
4	FERRARI	37
5	LIGIER	29
6	BENETTON	19
7	TYRRELL	11
8	LOLA	6
9	BRABHAM	2
10	ARROWS	1

Johnny Dumfries was recruited to drive alongside Ayrton Senna at Lotus after the Brazilian vetoed Derek Warwick's inclusion as a member of the team.

Alan Jones and Patrick Tambay were now embarked on a full season with the new Carl Haas Lolas after a pilot effort at the end of the previous year. With a new Ford V6 turbo scheduled to be ready for Imola, the Haas Lolas were running the first few races of the season using Brian Hart's four-cylinder turbo, which had originally entered F1 back in 1981 with Toleman.

Spain rejoined the world championship calendar with the second race of the season staged at the brand new Jerez autodrome, deep in sherry-producing country near Seville. This was the race in which Mansell proved he was a match for Piquet in equal cars, erupting back into contention after a late race tyre stop to pass the chequered flag alongside Ayrton Senna's pole-winning Lotus 98T. Officially timed at one-hundredth of a second, it was the closest grand prix finish since Peter Gethin's BRM pipped Ronnie Peterson's March by a similar margin some 15 years earlier in the Italian Grand Prix. Piquet retired with engine problems, leaving Prost third in his McLaren-TAG.

The McLaren team began the season looking rather vulnerable, with a sizable gap between their qualifying potential and that of the dauntingly powerful Hondas in spite of the McLaren's superior chassis. But there was much more of a premium this year on sensitive and economical driving under the 1986 fuel regulations, and Prost proved himself an absolute master of this technique when he won the San Marino Grand Prix, judging things so finely that his McLaren began to stutter for lack of fuel on the run up to the chequered flag.

Piquet was outdistanced in second place on this occasion, with Berger's Benetton third ahead of Johansson in the Ferrari. Prost already led the championship table, three points clear of Senna, and he followed that up by simply destroying the opposition at Monaco, Keke Rosberg vainly trying to keep him in sight to round off an impressive McLaren 1-2. Senna could not conceal his frustration at finishing an outclassed third, while Mansell struggled home fourth, hampered by poor engine response out of the tight corners. Prost now had two wins out of three races and kept his advantage in the title chase.

In the Brabham camp, the first few races had gone badly. Designer Gordon Murray had laid his reputation on the line with the striking low-line BT55 which, with its special angled-over BMW engine and seven-speed gearbox, was intended to produce significantly less aerodynamic drag than its rivals. Unfortunately it was an over-complex machine which never quite realised its potential; and it was to be associated with tragedy. While testing at Paul Ricard during the week following the Monaco Grand Prix, Elio de Angelis crashed one of the BT55s at very high speed and died from his injuries. The popular Roman had left Lotus at the end of the previous season, seeking a fresh challenge with a new team, as he was unwilling to take second billing to Senna. His place in the Brabham line-up was taken by Derek Warwick, who had been thrown out of F1 work when the Renault team closed its doors for the last time at the end of the previous season.

As an index of Senna's determination to mould Team Lotus to suit his own personal ambitions, the Brazilian had vetoed Warwick's inclusion in the team as he was not convinced of Lotus's capacity to field two competitive cars, or of results-starved Warwick's willingness to fulfil a supporting role. In the event, F3 graduate Johnny Dumfries was taken onto the team strength, but Senna soon found out that his biggest problem was his Renault engine. Although he planted the Lotus 98T on pole position no fewer than nine times during the course of the year, the French V6 did not stand comparison with Honda in the performance/fuel-economy stakes. Frustrated at the lack of usable race power, he had to sit behind in second place at Spa, watching Nigel Mansell pick up victory in the Belgium Grand Prix after Piquet's engine expired. Johansson finished third in Belgium, overtaking Alboreto against team orders. The Italian had opted for a non-stop run without a tyre stop, but Stefan's strategy of changing to fresh rubber was shown to be the correct decision. Michele was distinctly unamused.

Prost supreme

That Belgian GP was one of Prost's most outstanding races, even though it only netted

him sixth place. Enmeshed in a first-corner collision, his McLaren was launched high into the air, crashing down into the circuit with a deranged nose section and engine mounts so badly damaged that the chassis was left badly out of alignment. It was not simply that he made up a lot of ground during the course of the race that impressed the whole McLaren team, but that he did so without once ever touching the boost control. By contrast, Rosberg wound the boost up dangerously high as he battled to claw back time, paying the price with an almost inevitable engine breakage.

Nigel Mansell was now growing in confidence with each race. At the Canadian Grand Prix in Montreal he planted his Williams on pole position and led throughout, beating Prost, Piquet and Rosberg in a performance that catapulted him up to equal second with Senna, behind Prost in the championship stakes. But on the following weekend Senna leaped to the top of the ratings after a splendidly judged victory at Detroit, his inch-perfect precision between those concrete barriers more than making up for any power deficiency in his engine. Laffite's Ligier finished a strong second from Prost (who hates the place), while Mansell faded to fifth with brake trouble after leading briefly.

On his return to Europe, Mansell proved simply scintillating. His confidence running at a high level, he now began consistently to eclipse team-mate Piquet, which caused some tension within the Williams team. Nelson believed that his F1 status should preclude him from having to compete with Mansell, who should play a supporting role and defer to him on the circuit whenever necessary. But, while nobody in the Williams camp had really believed that Nigel was going to blossom into such an astoundingly effective grand prix winner, neither were they going to place any constraints on his performance. If Nelson wanted to beat him, he'd better do it out on the circuit.

At Paul Ricard for the French Grand Prix, Williams designer Patrick Head calculated that his drivers would be best served by making two scheduled stops for fresh rubber, as compared with the single stop anticipated by McLaren. The strategy worked perfectly, with Mansell dominating the race and Prost getting ahead only when the Williams came in for new tyres. Piquet, obviously flustered, had a spin and could only finish third. Alain finished second, but with Senna spinning off on an oil slick on the third lap, Mansell had now closed to within

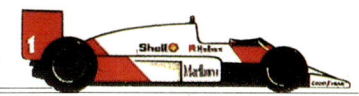

a point of the Frenchman at the head of the world championship table, heading for the British Grand Prix on the crest of a wave of confidence.

Brilliance at Brands

Piquet pipped the Englishman for pole at Brands Hatch and accelerated away from the grid, apparently dashing Mansell's hopes of another home win. Nigel's Williams broke a driveshaft, but even as he was pulling to one side, a multiple pile-up among the second half of the grid going into Paddock Bend brought the red flags out, giving Nigel the chance of a re-start at the wheel of the spare FW11. Sadly, while Christian Danner's Arrows, Allen Berg's Osella and Piercarlo Ghinzani's similar car were unable to take the re-start, Jacques Laffite's Ligier hit a barrier head-on, seriously injuring his legs in an accident which finished the veteran Frenchman's F1 career for good, although he later made a complete recovery.

At the re-start Piquet went ahead, with Berger briefly poking his Benetton through into second place while Mansell got used to the handling of his new mount, which had been set up for Piquet: one of the perks of being team leader! But Nigel was soon up onto Nelson's tail and when the Brazilian missed a gear, darted through into the lead. Mansell came out from his routine tyre stop just ahead of his number one and, willed on by the crowd, stayed ahead long enough to pick up the pace once again. Thereafter the fans were treated to an epic chase with Mansell breaking Piquet's challenge to win a truly momentous victory, his success made all the more memorable by the fact that the spare Williams-Honda had no drinks bottle and Nigel finished dehydrated.

Almost unnoticed, Prost's McLaren-TAG was a steady third, lapped by the victorious Williams-Hondas, while René Arnoux's Ligier was fourth. Martin Brundle backed up a great result for Britain with fifth for Tyrrell, while Johnny Dumfries was seventh and Derek Warwick a disappointed eighth. His Brabham had held fifth place with four laps to go when it ran short of fuel and spluttered back out of the points, much to the Hampshire driver's frustration.

Piquet was determined to counter-attack and regain the initiative, which he did admirably at Hockenheim to win the German Grand Prix comfortably after a tight battle with Rosberg's McLaren, which had qualified on pole. Both Keke and Alain Prost ran short of fuel, misled by faulty onboard computer read-outs, while Mansell finished third behind Senna, complaining of a high-speed handling imbalance which was traced to loose screws retaining the aerodynamic diffuser panel under the gearbox.

Now it was Mansell's turn to feel the draught. When the action moved behind the Iron Curtain to the first Hungarian Grand Prix to be staged at the magnificent Hungaroring track a few miles outside Budapest, Piquet won again after a battle with Senna's tenacious Lotus-Renault. Nigel was an annoyed third, absolutely convinced that Nelson had misled him over the performance of an experimental differential which the Brazilian had tried in practice. The team

Nigel Mansell and Nelson Piquet prepare for battle against the rest – and against each other – as their Williams-Hondas line up in the pit lane prior to the British GP at Brands Hatch. Nigel came top this time.

177

Gerhard Berger enjoyed a non-stop run to victory in the Mexican GP, his Benetton's Pirelli tyres providing a distinct advantage on this occasion as the Goodyear runners were plagued with serious wear problems.

attempted to pour oil on slightly troubled waters but were brought up with a start at Österreichring, where both drivers retired from the Austrian Grand Prix, allowing Prost to win by a lap from Alboreto's Ferrari. The Lola-Fords of Alan Jones and Patrick Tambay enjoyed their best results of a generally undramatic season, finishing fourth and fifth behind Johansson's Ferrari. Christian Danner, who had switched from Osella to Arrows after Marc Surer was badly injured in a rallying accident mid-season, took the first point of his career with sixth place.

Monza was next. Piquet beat Mansell fair and square in the Italian Grand Prix, but the Brazilian's swerving at his number two as he overtook made the biggest impression on Nigel. Clearly, he could ask for no favours from the Brazilian; moreover, Honda were known to want Nelson to take the championship. The Englishman had a five-point advantage over him with three races to go, but Prost was still a threat, and even Senna had an outside chance.

Ayrton finally found himself out of contention when he ran out of fuel and dropped to fourth place in the Portuguese Grand Prix, which Mansell led from start to finish to beat Prost and Piquet across the line. It was prob-

ably the best and most dominant performance of his career to date, but all the effort seemed to have evaporated when he failed to have the car in gear at the start of the Mexican Grand Prix and was swamped by the rest of the field.

The high-altitude central American event, returning to the calendar after an absence of 16 years, was held on the slightly revamped but still very bumpy Autodromo Hermanos Rodriguez in the Magdelena Mixhuca park complex close to the centre of Mexico City. Gerhard Berger profited by running non-stop on particularly suitable Pirelli rubber to achieve the Benetton team's first Grand Prix triumph, Prost keeping his title hopes open by finishing second ahead of Senna, Piquet and Mansell.

It is a matter of history now that Williams fumbled their championship chances under the watchful eye of Sochiro Honda himself in the final race of the season at Adelaide, Australia. Mansell had it perfectly weighed up, running smoothly in third place behind Piquet and Prost. Keke Rosberg had set the pace from the start, having decided to retire at the end of the season and wanting to make his final race for McLaren a memorable one. But he was duped into retiring with a disin-

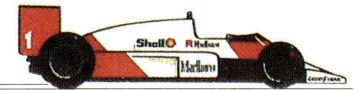

tegrating tyre, thinking the vibration was due to engine failure.

Mansell could almost taste the victory champagne when a rear tyre exploded on his Williams and he just managed to keep the wayward car under control long enough to bring it to a halt. Now it seemed to be

Piquet's championship but Nelson was called in for a precautionary and, as it turned out, unnecessary pit stop. He resumed in second place behind Prost, but time had run out. Alain won the race, to become the first to retain the world championship since Sir Jack Brabham in 1960!

Alain Prost won the Australian GP to clinch his second successive drivers' title. **Inset** *Prost on the rostrum with Nelson Piquet (second) and Stefan Johansson (third).*

1987

Piquet's third Championship: turbos muzzled with pop-off valves: Berger wins for Ferrari: Barnard joins Maranello

FISA chose to go a step further in 1987, retaining the 195-litre fuel capacity maximum, but also requiring the turbo brigade to fit its engines with boost-control valves, with a limitation of 4-bar pressure. This brought maximum power down to around the 900bhp mark and was intended to end the practice of developing sacrificial engines capable of putting out 1200bhp just for a few qualifying laps.

Driver changes included Gerhard Berger going to Ferrari, his place at Benetton taken by Thierry Boutsen. With Rosberg's retirement, former Ferrari driver Stefan Johansson took up the number two McLaren seat alongside Prost, Martin Brundle left Tyrrell for Zakspeed, swapping places with Jonathan Palmer. Japanese driver Satoru Nakajima joined Senna at Lotus, the British team's new car now using Honda turbo-power instead of Renault.

There was a separate class for non-turbo cars in the Championship for the first time, drivers and constructors respectively competing for the Jim Clark and Colin Chapman trophies. And, in a further attempt to narrow the performance margin between the two types of engine, the non-turbos had a 500kg minimum weight limit (540kg for the turbos) and no constraints on fuel capacity.

At McLaren there had also been changes in the design department, technical director John Barnard having departed to Ferrari the previous autumn. But his former protégé Steve Nichols did a good job putting the finishing touches to the McLaren MP4/3 and, when Alain Prost kicked off with yet another victory in the Brazilian Grand Prix, it seemed possible that the TAG-engined machines were set for a fourth consecutive season of front-line success.

1987 DRIVERS' CHAMPIONSHIP

		points
1	Nelson Piquet	73
2	Nigel Mansell	61
3	Ayrton Senna	57
4	Alain Prost	46
5	Gerhard Berger	36
6	Stefan Johansson	30
7	Michele Alboreto	17
8	Thierry Boutsen	16
9	Teo Fabi	12
10	Eddie Cheever	8
11	Satoru Nakajima	7
	Jonathan Palmer	7
13	Riccardo Patrese	6
14	Andrea de Cesaris	4
	Philippe Streiff	4
16	Derek Warwick	3
	Philippe Alliot	3
18	Martin Brundle	2
19	René Arnoux	1
	Ivan Capelli	1
	Roberto Moreno	1

CONSTRUCTORS' CHAMPIONSHIP

		points
1	WILLIAMS	137
2	McLAREN	76
3	LOTUS	64
4	FERRARI	53
5	BENETTON	28
6	ARROWS	11
	TYRRELL	11
8	BRABHAM	10
9	LOLA	3
10	ZAKSPEED	2
11	LIGIER	1
	MARCH	1
	ATS	1

However, on the strength of the previous season's results, Honda-powered cars looked like being the strongest contenders, and a great deal was expected of the new Lotus 99T penned by Gérard Ducarouge. Fitted with Lotus's computer-controlled active suspension, the team hoped it would give Senna an edge over Mansell and Piquet, but things did not quite work out that way. From the first race Senna realised that his car was not as fuel-efficient as the Williams FW11B owing to inferior aerodynamics, and that he could never compete on even terms. Moreover, the Lotus was heavier than the Williams.

The season started with familiar echoes of 1982: the threat of a drivers' strike at Rio, the bone of contention this time being the 'sliding-scale' tariff imposed by FISA for the issue

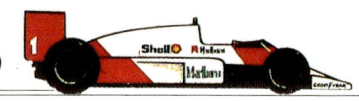

of F1 super-licences. However, just as at Kyalami in 1982, the race went ahead, with Mansell and Piquet on the front row ahead of Senna and Teo Fabi's Benetton, now fitted with Ford Cosworth power.

Mansell fumbled his start, so Piquet led initially before Senna took a turn. But Prost's careful strategy would see the McLaren driver get through on two tyre stops rather than his rivals' three, Piquet winding up a disgruntled second with Stefan Johansson opening his McLaren account with a fine third place, despite suffering from fumes in the cockpit.

Senna's Lotus stopped with engine failure, but the Brazilian had seen enough to realise his would be an uphill struggle in 1987; Berger, on the other hand, started his Ferrari career with fourth place, ahead of Boutsen's Benetton-Ford and a delayed Mansell.

Mansell then returned to Europe and drove faultlessly to win the San Marino Grand Prix at Imola, on this occasion not having to worry about any threat from his team-mate after Piquet crashed his Williams-Honda heavily during qualifying. Badly shaken up, Nelson did not take part in the race. And when responsibility for the accident seemed to stem from a slight change in tyre specification for this race, Goodyear very responsibly withdrew all the suspect covers and replaced them overnight—a logistical marathon which involved a chartered jet shipping new supplies in from England. The French Ligier team started its season at Imola, having missed Rio after they had fallen out with Alfa Romeo over its new and obviously uncompetitive turbo. The Italian company

used Arnoux's outspoken comments on the matter as an excuse to pull out, leaving Ligier quickly to conclude a deal for BMW-derived Megatron engines in order to go racing.

Despite Senna easing him out of pole position, Mansell never had any real worries in the race, winning comfortably from Ayrton, who spent much of his time battling for second place with Alboreto's Ferrari that eventually finished third. Johansson was fourth, ahead of Martin Brundle's Zakspeed, with Nakajima taking his first point with sixth. Prost was an early retirement with alternator problems. He was running second and starting to edge closer to Mansell at the time, feeling very confident.

Prost extends his lead

The cool, calculating Frenchman was destined to profit from the impetuosity of his colleagues when the action moved to Spa for the Belgian Grand Prix, for although Mansell's chilling commitment and speed earned him pole position ahead of Piquet, he found himself facing the pressure of a second start after the Tyrrells of Palmer and Philippe Streiff were comprehensively destroyed in a first lap accident at the fast and tricky Eau Rouge corner.

Mansell had led commandingly from the first start, but when Senna's Lotus burst through to take the initiative at the second, Nigel's impatience bubbled over recklessly. Mid-way round the opening lap, he attempted an unnecessarily precarious overtaking manoeuvre, the two cars touched and spun off. Senna was unable to

Ayrton Senna scored a fortunate victory in the Monaco GP, at the wheel of the active-suspension Lotus 99T-Honda, after Nigel Mansell, with a commanding lead, was forced to retire.

retrieve his Lotus from a sand trap, and although Mansell resumed, accident damage eventually caused him to stop. An unruly scuffle then followed in the Lotus garage as Mansell took up the matter with Senna, the Englishman seemingly unable to suppress an impulsive response when confronted with his rival.

All this played into Prost's hands, of course. Piquet led briefly until his Williams-Honda suffered an engine problem, after which the Frenchman headed Johansson to the finish in majestic 1-2 formation. The two men finished the afternoon at the head of the Championship, five points apart.

Monaco followed with Mansell performing faultlessly in qualifying to take pole position, then pulling out a commanding lead in the race before retiring with a cracked exhaust. Senna thus inherited an easy win from a lacklustre Piquet, who was still feeling stale and jaded, the after-effects of his Imola accident taking some time to pass. Third and fourth were the two Ferrari F187s, Alboreto heading Berger.

The Italian driver performed well after an unnerving and very spectacular practice collision with Christian Danner's Zakspeed on one of the fastest parts of the circuit. The German was held responsible for the incident and barred from any further part in the weekend's proceedings—a sanction which even Alboreto regarded as too harsh. Jonathan Palmer did well to finish fifth for Tyrrell ahead of Ivan Capelli's March.

Now it was Senna's turn to take over at the head of the Championship table with his second straight win over the bumpy streets of Detroit, this time after Mansell dropped back with severe leg cramps after qualifying on pole and leading the early stages. Piquet

Jonathan Palmer heads to fifth place – and the first Championship points of his career – in the Monaco GP.

picked up second place from Prost, with Berger fourth from the pained Mansell and Eddie Cheever's Arrows. Nakajima's Lotus proved the worth of the newly developed on-board TV camera system when he collided with Capelli's March and Adrian Campos's Minardi in an action-packed opening lap which was beamed all round the world!

The Canadian Grand Prix did not take place this year owing to a dispute between potential race sponsors, so now it was back to Europe for the French Grand Prix at Paul Ricard, which turned out to be one of those familiar two-horse races between the Williams-Hondas. Mansell lunged ahead of Piquet mid-race in a breathtakingly audacious overtaking manoeuvre, after which the Brazilian gambled, incorrectly, that a second change of tyres would enable him to catch his team-mate and rival. Prost finished third ahead of Senna, the Lotus driver maintaining his position at the head of the title chase, one point ahead of Prost.

In the run-up to the British Grand Prix Mansell and Williams looked outwardly as though they were strengthening their World Championship hand, but behind the scenes some intensive politicking was taking place. Piquet was getting increasingly annoyed over Williams' continued unwillingness to impose any sort of obligation on Mansell to play second fiddle; and when Nigel recovered from an unscheduled tyre stop to pip him for victory in the British Grand Prix less than three laps from the chequered flag, it was quite simply the last straw.

The Brazilian began to cast around for a new team in 1988, a course of action which would, obliquely, lose Williams its Honda engine supply for the following year. At the same time Senna, whose Lotus had finished a lapped third at Silverstone ahead of Nakajima's sister car, knew that he had to leave the Hethel team if he was to have any realistic chance of winning the Championship. The third strand to this complex plot was McLaren's realisation, graphically brought home to Prost at Silverstone, that the TAG turbo was fast becoming eclipsed by its Japanese rivals.

Piquet wins at last

Against this backcloth of complex dealings behind closed doors, Nelson Piquet strengthened his Championship chances with a lucky first win of the season at Hockenheim, inheriting the lead in the German Grand Prix with only five laps left to run after Prost's

seemingly resurgent McLaren-TAG retired when its alternator drive-belt broke. Mansell by this time was already out with engine failure, so Johansson's McLaren took a dramatic second place, its right front tyre in shreds for the final half-lap. Senna was third, struggling home after an hydraulic fluid leak had caused his Lotus's active suspension to collapse onto its emergency springs. By the end of the weekend he had decided to leave Lotus. Although it was still top secret, Ayrton would join McLaren alongside Prost for 1988—and the team would have Honda engines.

The moment Lotus got wind of this, they acted with commendable speed to retain their Honda engine deal. They announced Nakajima's retention as second driver, then quickly concluded a deal with Piquet to be their number-one driver. Thus, by the Hun-

garian Grand Prix, Williams were seemingly out on a limb. Piquet would continue the year to win the Championship and Williams would then lose their Honda engines, obtaining generous severance terms from the Japanese company which would enable them to finance an alternative source of engine supply the following year.

The Hungarian Grand Prix must have made Mansell believe he was fated never to win a World Championship. Qualifying on pole, he had the race in the bag, only for a wheel retaining nut to work loose. He lurched to a disbelieving halt out on the circuit and Piquet won from Senna. Ferrari's challenge strengthened at this race, with Berger qualifying on the front row and running second before transmission failure intervened. Prost was third and Boutsen a smooth fourth with the Benetton-Ford.

*The atmosphere for the British GP was electrifying after the two Williams-Hondas had battled for the lead at Paul Ricard a week earlier (**inset left**). Mansell won at Silverstone, despite a pit stop (**inset right**), although he had to fight his way past Prost's McLaren (No. 1, **main picture**) on the first lap to get a crack at Piquet.*

183

Above *The Arrows A10Bs of Derek Warwick and Eddie Cheever run in close company during the early laps of the Austrian GP.*

It took three attempts—and two startline accidents—before the Austrian Grand Prix got successfully underway, highlighting concern over the lack of width at the Österreichring start/finish line which would result in the race being dropped from the fixture list the following year. Piquet led away initially, Mansell holding back in fourth as he allowed his overworked clutch to cool down. Once that had been accomplished, he caught and passed Nelson with contemptuous ease, winning by almost a minute. Fabi and Boutsen were third and fourth for Benetton.

Before Monza, the axe fell to sever the Williams/Honda alliance, the English team confirming it would use Judd naturally aspirated engines on a weekend when Senna's switch to McLaren-Honda also became public knowledge. Mansell now felt that the tide was running against his World Championship chances, particularly when Piquet used the Williams computer controlled 'reactive' suspension system to gain a performance edge in that weekend's Italian Grand Prix.

In fairness, Nelson won only after Senna slid off the road briefly with a handful of laps to go, the Lotus driver unsuccessfully gambling on running non-stop without a tyre change. Mansell was third beind Senna; Berger was fourth in front of Boutsen and Johansson. Off-track, the FISA Medical Commission hinted strongly that it was seriously considering imposing drug tests in motor racing, although primarily as a precaution to head-off a problem which had not infact reared its head to any measurable extent in this particular sport.

Mansell's championship was slipping away now and even he could feel it. He

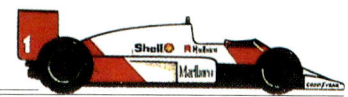
began to become slightly concerned about the specification of the engines he was allocated by Honda, convinced that Nelson was being favoured now that he and Williams were, long-term at least, outcasts from the Japanese fold. This concern turned seemingly to paranoia after the Portuguese Grand Prix at Estoril, where his engine mysteriously cut out a handful of laps into the race, causing his retirement. On the car's return to the paddock, the V6 fired immediately: it had been a minor electrical fault!

Not that Piquet benefitted unduly from Mansell's misfortune on this occasion: he finished third. The race was dominated from the start by Berger's Ferrari. But under relentless pressure from the pursuing Prost, Gerhard had been flustered into a spin close to the finish, allowing the McLaren driver to duck through to his 28th grand-prix win, and so to overtake Jackie Stewart's record of 27 victories which had endured since 1973.

Nigel's last two wins for Williams

Mansell countered with a tremendous victory in the Spanish Grand Prix at Jerez the following week, Prost and Johansson taking second and third places on this occasion while Piquet, who drove erratically, wound

up fourth ahead of Senna. Mansell was now 18 points behind Piquet with three races to go. He was going to need a lot of luck.

The Mexican Grand Prix turned out to be a two-part affair with an aggregate result, the event being interrupted when Warwick's Arrows crashed at high speed exiting the fast right-hander before the stare/finish line. It was thought that the car had suffered a suspension breakage, almost certainly weakened by an earlier incident when Nakajima's Lotus rammed it from behind. Mansell scored another crucial win, but Piquet was an extremely lucky second. He had been involved in a rare collision with Prost on the opening lap and, while the McLaren was eliminated on the spot, Nelson got the benefit of a push-start as his car was deemed to be in a hazardous position. Patrese's Brabham led the remainder of the depleted field home third from Cheever's surviving Arrows and Fabi's Benetton.

Mansell's championship challenge finally ended at Suzuka, venue for the first Japanese Grand Prix for a decade. Jousting for pole position with Piquet, he crashed heavily and was taken to hospital with unspecified back injuries. Within 24 hours he was being loaded aboard a Europe-bound Boeing 747, his title challenge spent. However, there was to be no fairy-tale victory for Honda on home soil. Piquet's Williams expired with an embarrassing, and major, engine failure, while Gerhard Berger romped to a long-overdue Ferrari triumph, putting the Prancing Horse back on the victory rostrum for the first time in over two years. Senna pipped Johansson for second place on the last lap while Alboreto climbed through to fourth in the other Ferrari, having lost the use of his clutch on the starting grid and completed the first lap in last place.

All that was left was the Australian Grand Prix where Riccardo Patrese, already signed to replace the departing Piquet for 1988, was released by Brabham to join the Williams team one race early. In Riccardo's place, European F3000 champion Stefano Modena, winner of the Birmingham Super Prix, made his F1 debut in a Brabham BT56.

Berger led unchallenged from the first lap, Alboreto eventually being classified second after Senna's Lotus was disqualified for having excessively large brake-cooling ducts. Boutsen's Benetton was third, with Palmer taking the best result of his career with fourth for Tyrrell, ahead of recent arrivals Yannick Dalmas (LC Lola) and Roberto Moreno, who had replaced the painfully slow Pascal Fabre in the tiny AGS team.

Left Alain Prost hounds Gerhard Berger during practice for the Portuguese GP. In the race, they would have a re-run of this chase, Berger spinning off in the closing stages (but recovering to come second) and handing a record 28th career victory to Prost.

185

THE HONOURS

1988

McLaren-Honda break all the records with 15 wins from 16 races: Senna's title with record eight wins as turbo era ends

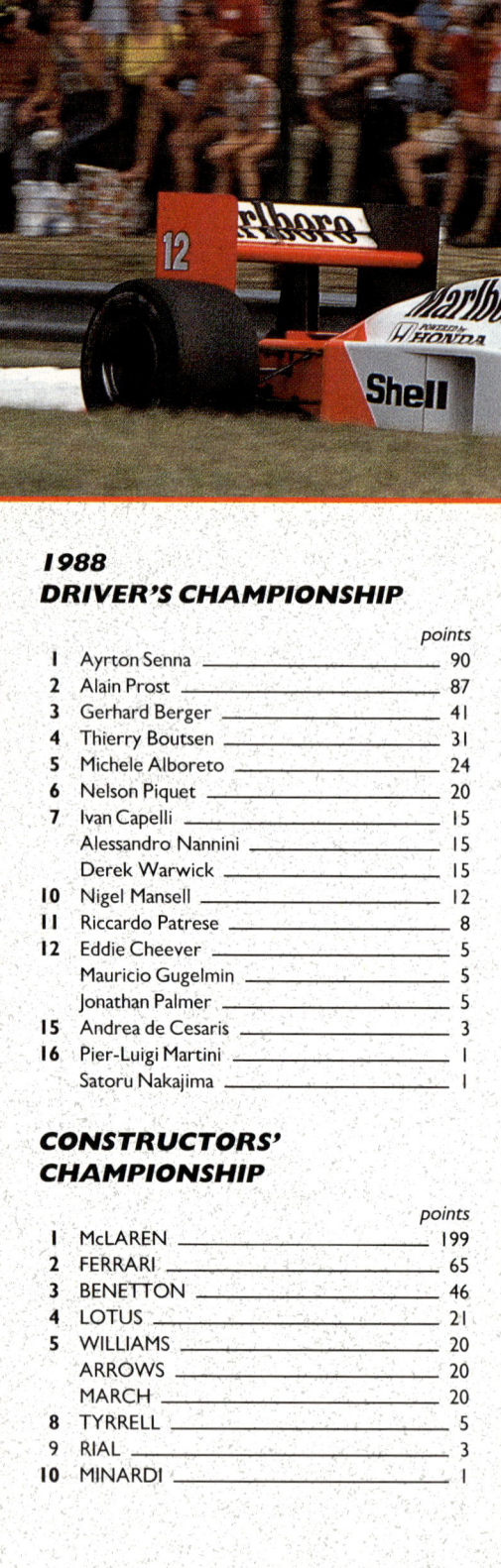

Right Senna in stylish action on his way to yet another McLaren-Honda victory at the Hungaroring.

For those with memories long enough to recall the spluttering early efforts of Renault's F1 turbo, the manner in which the era of forced-induction grand-prix engines came to a close in 1988 had as much in common with those pioneering days 12 years earlier as a Concorde has with a Dakota. Yet nobody could have anticipated that the McLaren-Hondas would be honed to display such an embarrassingly complete level of domination.

For the final turbo season, FISA was determined that the naturally aspirated brigade would at last get on competitive terms. To this end, they cut boost pressure to 2.5 bar and fuel capacity to a parsimonious 150 litres. But Honda's technical ingenuity produced something in excess of 650bhp from their familiar V6, and this, allied to the wonderfully competitive McLaren MP4/44 chassis and brilliant driving by Prost and Senna proved more than sufficient to get the job done. Moreover, at these relatively low levels of mechanical stress, the Honda engines demonstrated almost bullet-proof reliability throughout the year.

Lotus, although equipped with identical power units, had a simply appalling time. Ducarouge's new type 100T turned out to be a dud and Nelson Piquet's motivation seemed to take a holiday. Although Gerhard Berger and Michele Alboreto would score an emotionally loaded victory in the Italian Grand Prix at Monza, it was a later-race success made possible only by Senna tripping over back-marker Jean-Louis Schlesser.

The regulations permitted turbo teams to use uprated versions of the 1987 cars if they wished, but for naturally aspirated contenders and any turbo teams building a new car, stringent new constructional require-

1988 DRIVER'S CHAMPIONSHIP

		points
1	Ayrton Senna	90
2	Alain Prost	87
3	Gerhard Berger	41
4	Thierry Boutsen	31
5	Michele Alboreto	24
6	Nelson Piquet	20
7	Ivan Capelli	15
	Alessandro Nannini	15
	Derek Warwick	15
10	Nigel Mansell	12
11	Riccardo Patrese	8
12	Eddie Cheever	5
	Mauricio Gugelmin	5
	Jonathan Palmer	5
15	Andrea de Cesaris	3
16	Pier-Luigi Martini	1
	Satoru Nakajima	1

CONSTRUCTORS' CHAMPIONSHIP

		points
1	McLAREN	199
2	FERRARI	65
3	BENETTON	46
4	LOTUS	21
5	WILLIAMS	20
	ARROWS	20
	MARCH	20
8	TYRRELL	5
9	RIAL	3
10	MINARDI	1

ments for additional frontal protection were incorporated. McLaren none the less chose to build a brand new chassis, while Ferrari opted for an uprated version of the F187 which had won the last two races of the previous season.

Meticulous attention to detail characterised the McLaren team's approach, the

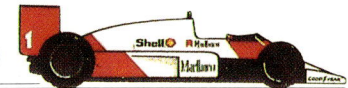

whole engine/chassis/driver package being superior in most respects, and the overall effect being to achieve what, even before the first race, appeared to be a commanding advantage. But the team was also extremely good at keeping its problems under wraps (there were several races, notably Canada, Portugal and Spain, for instance, where the engineers were extremely concerned that their competitive fuel consumption might be right on the margins). But, thanks often to the inability of the opposition to pose any consistent threat, the McLarens emerged unscathed. At the end of the year they clinched the Constructors' title by an enormous margin of more than 100 points.

The Senna-Prost show

The rivalry between Prost and Senna was also fascinating to observe at close quarters, probably the two most gifted drivers of their day shaping up to each other in identical cars. It was clear from the moment he took pole position at Río for the first race of the year that Senna was quicker; but after a crash at Monaco and problems with fuel consumption at Mexico, he had managed to win only one of the first four races. Prost took the other three, convincing many observers that he would be a better bet for the championship, taken over the season as a whole.

However, Senna strung together a remarkable sequence of four successive victories in the British, German, Hungarian and Belgian Grands Prix, the first two of which were in torrential rain at Silverstone and Hockenheim. Prost freely conceded that he was too

old and canny to race hard in conditions of zero visibility, but when he bounced back into contention to win the Spanish and Portuguese races, Ayrton seemed flustered.

Finally, in a breathtaking title clincher at Suzuka, Senna stalled on the grid, but just managed to get going again to climb through the field and beat Prost into second place, thereby taking the title with record eighth win of the year. His success broke the record of seven wins established by Jim Clark in 1963 and equalled by Prost 21 years later. (Prost rounded off the year by winning at Adelaide, raising his personal total for the year to seven victories).

Of the opposition, Ferrari did best, but only inasmuch as they were on hand to pick up that lucky victory at Monza when the McLarens faltered. Berger drove heroically all year, fighting an uphill battle with horrendous fuel consumption, although the revised F187 chassis handled well enough and enabled him to clinch pole position at Silverstone with team-mate Alboreto alongside.

For the curly haired Michele, 1988 was a troubled year. Mid-season he knew that he would not be staying at Maranello the following year afterMansell was signed. Later he concluded what he thought was a deal with Williams, only for Frank to change his

Above Gerhard Berger and Michele Alboreto profit from rare McLaren misfortune to complete a wildly acclaimed 1–2 at Monza.

Above left Thierry Boutsen's Benetton laps René Arnoux's Ligier on his way to third place in the Japanese GP at Suzuka, behind the McLarens of Senna and Prost.

Above right Alessandro Nannini jousts with Piquet at Imola; the pair have just lapped Julian Bailey's Tyrrell. Nannini was one of the rising stars of the season; Piquet and the Lotus disappointed.

mind and opt to retain Patrese. The whole Ferrari effort was conducted amidst a mood of great concern for the health of the ailing Enzo Ferrari and, indeed, an historic era finally ended on 14 August when the Grand Old Man of motor racing finally passed on at the splendid age of 90 years.

Off-stage, there had been more than a few tensions at Maranello as the Commendatore approached the end of his life, reflecting a general uncertainty about how the team would be administered after he had gone. A naturally aspirated 3.5-litre V12 development was finalised by John Barnard as a parallel programme to the V6 turbo development, but by the time this car, originally intended for 1988, was complete, Barnard already had sufficient information to hand to start work on a brand new machine in anticipation of 1989. Time alone would tell what fruit there long-term plans would bear.

Benetton did well, Thierry Boutsen and new recruit Alessandro Nannini now powered by a 3.5-litre V8 Cosworth DFR engine in place of the previous year's V6 turbo. If there had been no McLaren-Hondas in the F1 equation, Boutsen would, in all probability, have ended up as World Champion. The smooth and stylish Belgian driver

sped to six third places during the course of the season—though he would later be disqualified from third on his home ground at Spa when a fuel sample taken from the car was found to contravene the required octane rating.

The new men

Nannini also shone from time to time, taking a strong third place at Silverstone; but it was his compatriot Ivan Capelli who made the biggest impression in the striking new Leyton House March 881. Powered by a Judd V8 engine, Capelli finished a strong second to Prost in the Spanish Grand Prix and later briefly poked the nose of his March ahead in Japan, the first time a non-turbo car had led a grand prix since Alboreto had won at Detroit five years earlier.

While Capelli consolidated his reputation as the brightest of the rising stars, Mansell and the Williams team had a disastrous year, their first in which they failed to produce a single win for 10 years. The season began with the Judd-engined FW12 equipped with computer-controlled reac-

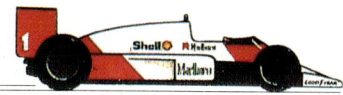

tive suspension, but this was soon deemed more trouble than it was worth and was replaced by a more conventional system after first practice at Silverstone. Mansell then stormed to second place in the British Grand Prix and had a similar encouraging run to take six points at Jerez, between which he missed two races after being stricken with a particularly virulent bout of chicken pox. His new team-make Patrese proved unspectacularly competent in the second car.

The Tyrrell team enjoyed an all-British line-up with Julian Bailey joining Jonathan Palmer at the start of the year, but their new car was a dismal performer and only Palmer's gritty determination hauled it to a handful of top-six placings during the course of the summer. Mid-season, John Barnard's colleague at Maranello, Englishman Harvey Postlethwaite, quit the Ferrari team to take over as Tyrrell technical director, a somewhat surprising decision which at least bodes well for better performances in the future.

Of the others, Arrows took the turbo route with their BMW-derived Megatron engines, but lacked the back-up and support of major manufacturer participation. Even so, Warwick and Cheever took several top-six placings and proved they were still drivers with which to be reckoned. Totally new teams on the scene included Rial (Andrea de Cesaris), Dallara (Alex Caffi) and EuroBrun (Stefano Modena and Oscar Larrauri). None of them made any great impression, while the established Ligier outfit went from bad to worse, veterans René Arnoux and Stefan Johansson failing to score a single point all season.

Thus ended the turbo era, a period of spectacular technical progress in grand-prix racing which spawned the fastest and most powerful F1 cars of all time. The way in which the major engine suppliers surmounted the enormously complex technical problems posed by this new generation of engines was quite remarkable, reflecting the tremendous investment of financial and manpower resources.

At the end of the day, there is not the slightest doubt that the turbo era in F1 conferred spin-off benefits to the world of road-going automobiles. Increased power with ever-improved fuel efficiency became a watchword which cut across the boundaries between motor racing and motor industry with incalculable benefits for both.

Above left Ivan Capelli drove brilliantly to finish second in the Portuguese GP at Estoril, particularly as it involved clawing past Ayrton Senna, whose McLaren is seen here hanging on ahead of the Italian's March 881.

Above right With a record eight wins out of 16 races, there was no denying Ayrton Senna's imperious claim to the driver's title.

189

INDEX

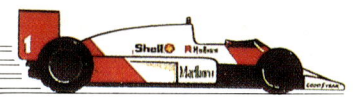